D0875277

# The Theory of Dumping and American Commercial Policy

# The Theory of Dumping and American Commercial Policy

**William A. Wares**
The University of Michigan

**Lexington Books**
D.C. Heath and Company
Lexington, Massachusetts
Toronto

**Library of Congress Cataloging in Publication Data**
Wares, William A
   The theory of dumping and American commercial policy.
   Bibliography: p.
   Includes index.
   1. Dumping (Commercial policy) 2. United States—Commercial
policy. I. Title.
HF1425.W37      382'.3'0973      76–54611
ISBN 0–669–01308–0

Published simultaneously in Canada

Printed in the United States of America

International Standard Book Number: 0–669–01308–0

Library of Congress Catalog Card Number: 76–54611

To my family, both central
and extended.

# Contents

# List of Figures and Table

# 1

# The Nature of Dumping and the Genesis of the United States Antidumping Act

The United States Antidumping Act was passed in 1921, and its substantive provisions have not been radically amended since that time.[1] The purpose of the Act was and is to regulate dumping in international trade to prevent the monopolization of domestic markets, thereby enhancing the welfare of the American people. To this end, the Act directs the Secretary of the Treasury to investigate complaints of dumping. When the Secretary believes that dumping may be occurring, he must suspend appraisement on all future imports of the merchandise in question. Moreover, if he chooses, he may withhold appraisement on all goods "entered, or withdrawn from warehouses, for consumption" up to 120 days prior to the initiation of the antidumping inquiry.[a]

Upon deciding that dumping is occurring, the Secretary of the Treasury must notify the International Trade Commission (ITC), and the ITC then investigates whether "an industry in the United States is being or is likely to be injured, or prevented from being established, by reason of" the dumping.[2] Should the ITC decide in the affirmative, antidumping duties are levied on all unappraised imports, and on all future imports that are dumped, in an amount equal to the dumping margin as defined in the Act. Furthermore, within this procedural framework, the Act gives the Secretary responsibility for promulgating any additional rules and regulations that are needed.

The Antidumping Act defines dumping as a situation in which an import's "fair value" exceeds the "purchase price" paid by the importer, or the "exporter's sales price," if the exporter or his agent markets the goods in the United States. According to the Act, the amount of antidumping duties must be equal to the difference between a good's "foreign-market value" and its purchase price or exporter's sales price, whichever is relevant in the case at hand. The Act describes how a good's purchase price, exporter's sales price, and foreign-market value are to be calculated, but it does not define a good's fair value. Consequently, the Secretary of the Treasury must construct the definition of this term.

---

[a] The provision on the withholding of appraisement presently contained in the Act is the result of an amendment included in the Trade Act of 1974. In addition to this and other significant revisions in the Antidumping Act, the Trade Act changed the name of the Tariff Commission to the International Trade Commission. *Trade Act of 1974, Statutes at Large* 88, sec. 171, 2009 (1974); and sec. 321 (a) 2043 (1974).

1

Moreover, the Act does not spell out the duties of the ITC, but merely indicates that the ITC must evaluate the effect of dumping. It does not define the meaning of "an industry in the United States." It does not describe what constitutes an injury, the likelihood of injury or the prevention of establishment; nor does it specify how the ITC is to determine whether an injury to a domestic industry occurs "by reason of" import dumping. Thus, the meaning of these terms has been left to the ITC. Although the ITC is not obligated to adhere to the principle of stare decisis, it has given these terms content through its discussion of the cases that have arisen over the years, rather than by establishing an inflexible body of rules.

In sum, United States commercial policy respecting dumping has four distinct aspects. The first aspect is an absence of regulations pertaining to the dumping of exports by American producers; the second, an administrative process for regulating import dumping; the third, a series of terms defining dumping and the dumping margin; and the fourth, a requirement that there must be an extant or prospective injury to an American industry for antidumping duties to be warranted. Of these features of present antidumping policy, the administrative process and the meaning of dumping have emerged from the provisions of the Antidumping Act and regulations established by the Secretary of the Treasury. The meaning of the injury requirement has been the product of case decisions made by the ITC.

In addition to the United States, many nations have enacted antidumping laws, and in 1967 the contracting parties to the GATT issued an antidumping code containing requirements for the proper regulation of dumping.[3] The GATT Antidumping Code is officially an elaboration of Article VI of the General Agreement, which concerns the topic of dumping. Since it is not an amendment to the agreement, contracting nations are not legally required to obey its directives. Nevertheless, because the GATT Code constitutes the accepted international standard for antidumping legislation, they are under a strong moral obligation to harmonize their policies with its dictates. With respect to the United States, commercial policy regarding dumping is in substantial agreement with the GATT Code, partly because Article VI was based on the American Antidumping Act, partly because the negotiators of the Code tried to avoid conflicts with the Act, and partly because of adjustments in Treasury Department policy since 1967. However, important areas of nonconformity remain.

In spite of the proliferation of national antidumping laws and the emergence of an international standard for such legislation, the economic literature contains little discussion of the impact of dumping on social welfare. In fact, a rigorous theory of the welfare effect of dumping has not been developed, and precise guidelines for formulating and criticizing antidumping policies do not exist. In turn, because of the absence of sufficient guidelines, the substantive provisions of the United States Antidumping Act have not been comprehensively evaluated since the Act's inception; and, although there have been some recent reforms in this aspect of the law, the most significant revisions have focused on administrative procedures.

Accordingly, this study has a twofold purpose: to construct a theory of the effect of dumping on national welfare, and to examine the United States Antidumping Act in the light of this theory. In the course of this endeavor, the basic questions that are answered are: (1) What does the theory of dumping suggest is the optimal manner in which to regulate this practice? (2) Do the provisions of the Antidumping Act comply with the dictates of economic theory on how dumping should be controlled? (3) Should American antidumping policy be revised to bring it into greater conformity with the international standards contained in the GATT Code?

With these questions in mind, the propriety of failing to regulate export dumping is investigated in Chapter 2. The economic theory of dumping as it pertains to the exporting nation is set forth therein. An appraisal is made of the welfare consequences of export dumping, and conclusions are drawn as to the optimal antidumping policy for the nation considered as an exporter. In Chapter 3, the arguments against import dumping that have been made in the past are analyzed, and the rationale for controlling dumping in import markets is distilled from the past criticisms of the practice. The manner in which dumping is defined and antidumping duties are computed under United States law is described and evaluated in Chapter 4. And in Chapter 5, recommendations for improving the Antidumping Act are offered, and the extent to which the GATT Code serves as a model for reform is inspected.

The purpose of the present chapter is to provide the reader with some general introductory information on dumping to aid in understanding the central issues noted above and the side issues that arise in the course of the study. The chapter contains four sections: a discussion of the meaning of the term ''dumping''; an explanation of the major causes of dumping; a short history of dumping prior to the enactment of the United States law; and a description of the factors that led to the passage of the Act. The final section brings together the main points of the discussion and elaborates on the nature and significance of the issues to be addressed in subsequent chapters.

## Dumping Defined

Economists define dumping as price discrimination in international trade; that is, the sale of like goods at different prices in two or more national markets. This general definition encompasses both price discrimination between the producer's home market and foreign markets and between export markets alone. It includes both the case in which the home price exceeds prices abroad and that in which it is lower.[4] Moreover, the definition emphasizes that dumping only differs from price discrimination in general in that national borders separate the relevant markets. Consequently, the theoretics of dumping and price discrimination will only differ if, for some reason, producers act differently in international as opposed to intranational trade. From the point of view of national policy, policymakers need only consider the welfare effects of the discrimination in one market when dumping occurs, whereas both markets must be considered when price discrimination is intranational.

When used correctly, the popular construction of the term has been narrower than its theoretical counterpart. In the import market, concern over dumping has primarily been exhibited by producers who felt their existence threatened by the low-priced foreign goods. They have labeled the practice "unfair" in the sense that the low-priced imports do not bear their "rightful" share of fixed costs, costs which import-competing producers must recoup on a pro-rata basis on their home sales. They have viewed the practice as predatory in the main, allowing foreigners to invade their markets by financing export sales at a loss through the accumulation of surplus profits from high-priced sales at home. Thus, in the market of importation, the concern of the most vocal interest group has been with dumping in which the import price is lower than the producer's home price.

This direction of price differentiation has also generated the greatest outcry in the producing country. In the home country, final consumers have historically charged that it is unfair for producers to burden them with a greater levy than the price at which foreign sales are found to be profitable.[5] When the low-priced export was a raw material or semifabricated input, advanced-stage industries consistently complained that the dumping placed them at a cost disadvantage, both in competing in foreign trade and in the domestic marketplace.[6] Consequently, in all markets, popular concern over selling at a lower price for export than for home use has predominated, and in the popular vernacular, "dumping" has been restricted to mean international price discrimination in this direction and between the home and foreign market. It has been saddled with connotations of "unfairness" and "predatory market invasion" and has thus been decried on moral as well as economic grounds.

National legislation has unanimously reflected this popular view of dumping. National laws against dumping have been justified in terms of the unfair and predatory nature of dumping sales. From their genesis in the early 1900s, national laws have been limited to prohibiting dumping when the import price is below the home price in the producing country. Offhand, this appears to be a somewhat anomalous practice since one would expect that legislators concerned with national welfare would be equally concerned with the foreign producer's ability to price monopolistically in their marketplace.

Jacob Viner, the most eminent student of dumping, fashioned his definition of the term to match its popular application. Within the general definition, he distinguished between "dumping proper" as the sale of similar goods at a lower price in export trade than at home, and "reverse dumping" as international price discrimination when the higher price is charged in exportation.[7] Because this is a useful distinction in discussing the theoretics of dumping and the United States legislation which is the subject of this study, I will adhere to Viner's nomenclature throughout.

Of course, the popular conception of dumping has not always been accurate. The term has often been used incorrectly and construed too broadly to include practices that do not involve price discrimination at all. Three important instances in which the term has been misused in this way are "surplus dumping," "social dumping," and "exchange dumping."

*Surplus Dumping*

The ideas of surplus production and dumping have frequently been associated in the popular mind. The practice of monopolists of exporting unexpected inventories at low prices to preserve the home market provides a legitimate basis for this association, but it does not explain the breadth with which the connection has been made. To some extent, the association may have originated in the idea that, in general, international trade innately involves the exportation of surpluses. For example, O. P. Austin wrote that "as a general axiom, nations do not begin to export until after home demand is satisfied." Modern technology makes it necessary to produce an output that exceeds home demand in order to achieve cost efficiency, and thus, "It might be said that, in its large volume, foreign trade is the purchase and sale of surpluses." Dumping, in turn, is merely an extension of this basic behavior. It is "the flooding of markets with cheap goods due to an unexpected amassing of surpluses that must be sold right away." It is, according to Austin, "an abuse of a nation's ability to export her surpluses."[8]

In fact, this usage was made of the term in the House Ways and Means Committee's report on Title I of the Emergency Tariff Bill of 1921, of which the United States Antidumping Act was Title II. Title I of the Bill proposed an increase in tariffs on agricultural imports, and a majority of the Committee claimed that the additional levies were needed because of the dumping of great quantities of foreign agricultural surpluses in the American marketplace. The dumpers, the majority noted, were industries with much lower costs than American producers, and thus American farmers could not feasibly become price competitive. No mention was made, however, of the relationship between import and foreign price levels, the allusion contained in the term "dumping" being solely to the low price of the imports compared to domestic costs of production.[9]

Similarly, in the congressional debate on the Antidumping Act, it was claimed that France was dumping war surplus material in the American market in spite of the fact that no market, and thus no market price, existed in Europe for these goods. Again, no reference was made to the home price of the goods in claiming dumping, only to their surplus status and low price.[10]

*Social Dumping*

Social dumping means the sale of imports at a price below that charged by competing domestic producers as a result of social conditions in the exporting country. Typically, in this view, low foreign wages, long working hours, extensive employment of female labor, or the like endow foreign producers with an unfair advantage in trade, and they subsequently "dump" cheap imports abroad.[11]

Since no price discrimination is engendered by the term, it seem obvious that social dumping is not dumping at all. Rather, if these and other elements of a country's social structure permit low-cost production, they are, in fact, the roots of the nation's comparative advantage, and the exports that they foster are no more "unfair" than those that would arise from superior technology. Thus, the concept of social dumping deserves summary dismissal.

In spite of the apparent vacuity of the concept, however, Representative Harter attempted to amend the Antidumping Act in 1935 to penalize social dumping. As described by Mr. Harter, the condition in need of rectification was that Japan, the Soviet Union, and other countries were producing goods at low cost because of the low wage rates and long working hours that existed in these nations. As a consequence, low-priced merchandise was being "dumped" in the American market and was injuring the American worker, who was entitled to a decent wage and could not be expected to compete with cheap foreign labor. The solution to this dilemma offered by Mr. Harter was to require the Secretary of the Treasury to issue a notice of dumping whenever goods were imported at a price less than the American cost of production, and subsequently to levy antidumping duties on such goods equal to the difference between these two figures. In requesting that the Antidumping Act be amended in this manner, Mr. Harter began his argument by stating, "This is not a plea for higher tariffs," although one is hard pressed to discover exactly why it was not.[12]

## Exchange Dumping

Exchange dumping is caused by the continual devaluation of a country's currency ahead of the rise in internal prices during a period of severe inflation. The persistent lag in the adjustment of internal prices to the external value of the domestic currency causes export prices to fall and remain low in terms of the currency of the importing nation. Clearly, the use of the appellation "exchange dumping" to describe the cheapening of imports in these circumstances is to be guilty of a misnomer once again. For exporters are not practicing price discrimination but are quoting identical prices on sales to foreign and domestic buyers alike.[13] The fall in export prices in terms of foreign currency values is incidental to their pricing policies, arising from their failure, usually unintended, to respond quickly to market forces beyond their control.

Nevertheless, concern over such dumping did play a minor part in the legislative history of the United States Antidumping Act. Immediately after World War I, it was feared that the drastic depreciation undergone by the Central European currencies had, in the manner described above, lowered the dollar value of imports and robbed the United States Treasury of customs revenue under the normal tariff. Consequently, the House Ways and Means Committee included in its antidumping bill a harsh measure designed to raise the levies on imports from nations with greatly depreciated currencies.[14] However, testimony before the Senate, indicated that export prices, denominated in the currency of the country of origin, had generally risen enough to offset external depreciation, and the Senate struck this proviso of the House bill.

## Causes of Dumping

Having defined the term with some precision, let us examine the economic conditions that give rise to dumping. Such conditions are two in nature: those that make dumping profitable and those that make it feasible.

With respect to motivation, regardless of the economics of the circumstances in which a firm finds itself, governments can make dumping a profitable policy. They can induce firms to dump by subsidizing exports, thereby lowering the private cost of production for foreign sale below the private cost of production for home consumption. Subsidies may be granted either directly in the form of bounties or indirectly through tax breaks, financial aid, or disproportionate rebates on raw material import duties. A government may institute these policies to create employment, correct a balance-of-payments deficit, develop a particularly valuable industry, or, archaically, on purely mercantilist grounds. Historically, government subsidization has been an important cause of dumping, with direct bounties responsible for the appearance of dumping in preindustrial times and indirect subsidies used to foster the practice in the late-nineteenth century.[15] Recently, the Soviet Union has gained reknown as a practitioner of subsidization whenever it lacks the foreign exchange required to fulfill its economic plans.[16]

Government subsidization aside, however, from the outset economists have linked the motivation to dump to the structure of the domestic market. The early authors who witnessed the dumping of American trusts, German cartels, and the syndicates of other European nations believed that dumping was beneficial to the absolute monopolist alone. F. W. Taussig wrote that "sales at lower prices are made to foreigners, not only sporadically, but for long periods and systematically. This phenomenon would seem to be explicable only on the grounds of monopoly."[17] Viner explained that in the late 1800s America's medium-sized firms did not dump because none could expect single-handedly to increase the home price by reducing domestic sales in this manner. Furthermore, any successful attempt to do so would confer a costless benefit on the dumper's rivals. On the other hand, small German firms could reap the rewards of international price discrimination because the establishment of cartels permitted them to raise domestic prices by dumping, and at the same time spread among all firms the burden of selling at lower prices abroad.[18] For this and other reasons Viner concluded that, in general, "it is only to a monopolist that export dumping has attractions greater than those of moderate domestic price cutting."[19] And as late as 1936, Gottfried von Haberler succinctly reiterated that "(a) necessary condition for dumping is monopoly upon the home market."[20]

Within the context of this viewpoint, Viner provided a comprehensive list of motives for dumping classified by the duration of dumping that each is likely to yield. While he stated that his categorization was not intended to be exhaustive and that alternative schemes of classification were possible, subsequent compilations, such as that of W. A. Seavy, have merely reworded Viner's work with little substantive addition.[21] Viner's classification is of interest because it has remained the basis for present-day legal commentary on dumping and, along with his arguments derived therefrom, has shaped current thinking on the subject. With some elucidation, it reads as follows:[22]

A. Motives for Sporadic Dumping
   1. Unintentional—dumping resulting from the receipt of a lower price than anticipated on the speculative foreign sale of goods.
   2. To dispose of a casual overstock—the dumping of unanticipated inventories in foreign markets rather than selling them at home and endangering the domestic price.
B. Motives for Short-run or Intermittent Dumping
   1. To maintain connections in a market where prices are, on remaining consideration, unacceptable—a potential pricing policy when the foreign market is temporarily depressed.
   2. To develop trade connections and buyers' goodwill in a new market.
   3. To eliminate competition—thereby acquiring monopoly power in a foreign market.
   4. To forestall the development of competition—and preserve monopoly power in the foreign market.
   5. To retaliate against dumping in the reverse direction—that is, against dumping by foreign-based rivals in the monopolist's home market.
C. Motives for Long-run or Persistent Dumping
   1. To maintain full production from existing capacity without cutting prices.
   2. To achieve economies of scale by increasing production without cutting prices—in this instance, capacity is increased precisely because the producer has the option to dump.

Because of the belief that dumping was a creature of monopoly, there arose a tendency to view dumping as a sign of restrictive, and perhaps illegal, business practices at home. In a study done for the Senate Temporary National Economic Committee in 1941, Milton Gilbert challenged the latter proposition and, indirectly, the former hypothesis as well.[23] Contrary to the views of prior authors, he found that systematic dumping was widely practiced by American industry. It was practiced by monopolists, oligopolists, and, in fact, even by monopolistic competitors who faced substantial competition in the home marketplace.[24] According to Gilbert, the reason that these weaker, imperfect competitors dumped was that, although they could utilize a variety of selling techniques at home—such as advertising and brand name identification—abroad they could often compete only on the basis of price.[25]

The works of J. Robinson and E. Chamberlin provide theoretical support for Gilbert's findings.[26] The authors show that any firm which has some control over its domestic price, however limited, will price above marginal cost. Thus, prices in foreign markets may exceed marginal cost even though they are below the home price, thereby making dumping a policy that maximizes short-run profits. Consequently, rather than being limited to monopoly, dumping is also the domain of any firm that possesses some ability to set prices at home, however slight.

When viewed with an eye to the precepts of marginalism, Viner's classification of motives reveals, in general, that such firms may engage in dumping for one of three basic reasons, each of which arises from a particular characteristic of monopolistic pricing: Because the home price is inordinately high in monopolistic markets, a producer may dump defensively to protect the domestic price against erosion. When the monopolistic seller earns abnormal profits on home sales, he may sell at a loss abroad to obtain future gains. Finally, the monopolistic producer may dump to maximize current profits when foreign prices fall within the range between the domestic price and marginal cost.

Conversely, on this basis, perfectly competitive firms will not engage in dumping because they lack motivation. A perfectly competitive firm cannot raise the price in any market by restricting sales, nor will an expansion of its sales lower the price. Thus, a perfect competitor does not have the power to acquire long-term gains by bringing about the demise of his rivals through temporary price cutting. Moreover, he will maximize his present profits if he disposes of his entire output at home or abroad depending on which market has the highest price net of transportation costs, and he will sell in both markets simultaneously only if the net price is the same in each.

Since it is the power to influence the home price that makes dumping a potentially advantageous policy, the amount of dumping that is likely to occur and the probable magnitude of the dumping margins involved will vary directly with the strength of a firm's monopoly position. The stronger the home monopoly, the greater will be the incentive to maintain home prices; the more frequently will foreign prices fall between the domestic price and marginal cost in production for home sale; and the larger will be the surplus profits, if any, that can be used to offset temporary losses abroad. Thus, monopoly and homogeneous or heterogeneous oligopoly are the market structures most conducive to dumping.

One set of economic conditions that fosters dumping, then, is those conditions that give rise to the monopolistic control of the home price or, alternatively, strengthen the monopolist's power in his home market. On the demand side of the market, a firm will have more effective monopoly power the more inelastic is its home demand curve, and thus goods that have few close substitutes, are necessities, or can be differentiated from rival products through advertising are likely candidates for discriminatory pricing in trade. On the supply side, the greater the financial, legal, organizational, and technological barriers to entry, the more likely is the establishment of monopoly. Consequently, dumping is particularly likely to occur in industries in which one or a few firms control a process or input essential to production or, as is more frequently the case, in which fixed costs are high and per-unit costs fall over a wide range of output.

In addition, monopoly may result from the formation of national or international cartels, in which case dumping is again exceedingly likely to ensue, although such dumping will probably be defensive rather than offensive. Firms can enforce a monopoly price through cartelization only because each member restricts its output. Each firm must refrain from selling the amount that it did previously at the lower, competitive price. And it must desist from selling additional output made profitable because the cartel price stands above the old level. Thus, a cartel necessarily creates excess capacity that could be profitably employed and an incentive for each member to cheat on the agreement. Consequently, cartels are likely to sanction dumping to relieve excess capacity and to encourage adherence to sales quotas in the monopolized market. In the same vein, international cartel arrangements may stipulate that member states forego previously important export sales made in each other's home markets. The subsequent search for alternative markets to maintain exportation may then result in dumping in the markets of nonmember states.[27] For example, in the mid-1960s the United States steel industry complained that just such an agreement between Japan and Western Europe had led these nations to dump extensively in the American marketplace.[28]

Besides obtaining an effective monopoly position at home, a firm must be protected against the resale of dumped goods in its home market if dumping is to be a feasible policy. Thus, the second necessary condition for international price discrimination is that reentry and resale must be precluded. High domestic tariffs have historically been conducive to dumping, both because they encourage domestic monopoly and because they serve as an impediment to the reentry of dumped goods.

In addition to high tariffs and other trade barriers, many aspects of the merchandise exported or of the transaction may serve to prevent reentry. Regarding the article traded, it may be perishable. It may be produced in slightly different styles which appeal to foreign but not domestic tastes. It may be a heavy or bulky, low-valued item subject to high per-unit transportation costs. Or, if an input, it may be sold at different stages of completion at home and abroad. With respect to the nature of the transaction, transportation costs may be high because the markets are distant. Supervision by the seller throughout the period of use may be possible, or the seller may only offer the article to known buyers who can be trusted. Furthermore, the buyer may have inadequate information on prices in different markets, or he may not possess the marketing organization or knowledge of foreign distribution channels necessary for resale.[29]

These, then, are the economic conditions and market structures that are amenable to dumping. In view of their nature, it is not surprising that much of the dumping that appears in the United States antidumping cases involves the sale of raw materials and semifabricated articles rather than finished goods. Inputs are usually more standardized than finished goods, and thus more susceptible to mass-production techniques which entail high fixed costs. They are likely to be produced in continuous-run plants where the costs of shutdown and changeover are great and the continuous use of capacity required. In terms of sources of supply, raw materials are likely to be owned and produced by a limited number of enterprises. Moreover, raw materials and semifabricated inputs will have a greater transportation cost relative to value because their selling price does not include markups and costs added in later stages of production. Thus, it may be expected that inputs, rather than finished output, will bear heavily in the traffic of dumping. It is not surprising, for example, that dumping has often occurred in the cement, steel, and chemicals industries.

### History of Dumping Before World War I

Before the proliferation of laws directly limiting the practice, dumping was relatively unfettered and could emerge whenever and wherever its prerequisites arose. Thus, the history of dumping before World War I followed closely the development of large-scale production and protective tariffs, on which basis it can be divided into three periods.[30]

The first period encompassed the mercantilist era that preceded the advent of modern technology and ended in the last quarter of the eighteenth century, when the effects of the Industrial Revolution began to appear. Because of the absence of large-scale production during this era, producers in every industry were too numerous to permit them to organize for the sake of raising domestic prices. There is some evidence that producers occasionally did unite for this purpose, and, as a means of reducing domestic supply, they granted bounties on exports in order to increase foreign sales. Except in a few instances, however, producers were unable to monopolize the home market and, consequently, they did not often dump on their own initiative. Rather, as mentioned above, in most cases they dumped in response to the export bounties that were a prominent feature of the mercantilist commercial policies of their governments. Thus, before the Industrial Revolution, dumping was the result of mercantilist policies aimed at acquiring a favorable balance of trade, not monopoly.

The second period extended from roughly the last quarter of the eighteenth century to the mid-nineteenth century. In the 1700s, governments had granted export bounties openly and directly, and, as a result, importing nations had encountered little difficulty in constructing tariff systems that nullified their effect. Consequently, by the start of the nineteenth century, governments had abandoned the general use of export bounties to encourage dumping.[31] By the American Revolution, however, Great Britain had begun to industrialize and adopt techniques of large-scale production, and her manufacturers had monopolized the domestic market in a number of industries. With the simultaneous existence of extensive customs duties, dumping inspired by monopoly self-interest arose as a practice of British manufacturers. Moreover, during the first half of the 1800s large-scale production was far more prevalent in Great Britain than elsewhere, and thus dumping continued to be almost exclusively the domain of British industry.[32]

Existing evidence suggests that British manufacturers dumped only occasionally during these years and did not dump as part of their normal price policy. Rather, the early instances of dumping were due to speculative miscalculation. And the purpose of dumping that was done throughout the remainder of the period was to maintain production in times of depression by meeting rival price cuts in competitive foreign markets. Thus, in the first half of the 1800s, dumping emerged as a monopoly pricing practice, but it was not continuous, predatory, or practiced by all nations.

In the third period, which ranged from roughly 1870 to 1914, the Industrial Revolution spread abroad. The emergence of large-scale production in Europe, the United States, Russia, and Japan reduced the number of firms in a variety of industries; as a result, all of the developing nations experienced some degree of monopolization. In most countries, syndicates appeared in only a few lines of manufacture; however, extensive cartelization occurred in Germany, and industrial trusts and corporate monopolies abounded in the United States. Moreover, with the exception of Great Britain, the manufacturing nations maintained significantly high tariffs between the late 1870s and World War I.[33] Consequently, their more concentrated industries turned to dumping with increasing frequency, and the practice became particularly widespread after 1890, when the monopolization of industry was no longer in its incipient stage.

With respect to the motives for dumping during this period, firms occasionally dumped to dispose of unanticipated surpluses. They were also willing to take short-run losses by dumping to maintain market connections or, when possible, to destroy foreign competition. However, most of the dumping between 1890 and World War I was done for the more enduring purpose of short-run profit maximization, and thus, in the main, monopolists dumped systematically and continuously as part of their normal pricing policies.

Of the industrialized countries, the United States and Germany emerged as the world's major dumping nations after 1870. In the United States, because antitrust laws forbade association for the purpose of controlling domestic prices, only firms that controlled a very large share of the domestic market engaged in dumping. Since market-dominating firms existed primarily in the staples and manufacturing specialties industries, American dumping was confined to these lines of production. Within these fields, however, dumping was a common, widespread practice, and such industrial giants as the American Harvester Company, the Standard Petroleum Company, and the United States Steel Corporation systematically and continually dumped for the purpose of increasing their export sales. In all, dumping by American monopolies involved several hundred products. It was responsible for the acquisition of a substantial portion of America's trade, and it caused the loudest outcry against dumping heard before World War I.

The cartel movement began in Germany in the 1870s. As elsewhere, industrialization increased competition and at the same time, by raising the capital cost of production, made the potential losses from market instability unacceptable. After the boom years of 1871-73, when prices fell and the severity of competition increased, German firms formed cartels to stabilize the domestic market. Tariffs passed in 1879 protected the neophyte cartels from foreign competition and, thereafter, they grew to such an extent that no important branch of German industry or export trade remained decentralized.[34]

The policy of the German cartels was to stabilize domestic prices at a level that exceeded world prices by the full amount of existing tariffs. Simultaneously, they used exports to maintain full-capacity production. In times of prosperity, domestic demand was occasionally great enough to utilize existing capacity, and only a small volume of exports was desired. Sufficient export sales could be obtained at domestic prices, so no dumping occurred. But this was true only in rare instances, for there was a chronic overexpansion of productive facilities in Germany between 1890 and 1914, and a substantial volume of exports was generally needed to maintain production in both prosperity and depression. The required volume of export trade could be acquired only by reducing prices below the domestic level and, consequently, systematic dumping was the normal price policy of the German cartels. Thus, while German producers dumped continually and were willing to dump to monopolize their export markets when it was feasible to do so, instances of predatory dumping were rare. Rather, the customary policy of the cartels was to prevent their members from exporting at prices lower than those necessary to dispose of excess output.

Privately motivated dumping, then, began in the late 1700s and was regularly practiced by industrialized nations for at least thirty years before World War I. Even as practiced by the United States and Germany, however, it was rarely engaged in for the purpose of monopolizing foreign markets, but was done continuously as one aspect of profit-maximizing export pricing. Consequently, in spite of its prevalence, only four nations passed statutes against dumping before 1914. Australia included an anti-dumping clause in a series of acts devoted to the problem of monopoly, New Zealand legislated against the dumping of a single line of goods, and only Canada and South Africa felt that dumping was worthy of a general legislative effort directed at preventing the problems that it created.[35]

By comparison, in the brief period from 1920 to 1922, no less than ten countries legislated against the practice, including Great Britain, tradi-tionally a free-trade nation. Moreover, after this time, the enactment of antidumping laws abruptly subsided, and only three more acts were passed in the remainder of the decade.[36] Thus, in the immediate postwar period, there was a sudden outburst of antidumping legislation that in-cluded the enactment of the United States statute in 1921. As this sug-gests, the origin of American commercial policy concerning dumping is to be found, less in a continual experience with the egregious effects of the practice, than in the anomalous economic and political conditions that fol-lowed World War I. For, in fact, the postwar environment was particular-ly conducive to the passage of legislation of this gender.

### Origins of the United States Antidumping Act of 1921

The first serious attempt to enact antidumping legislation in the United States actually occurred just before World War I, when the protariff forces of the Republican Party tried to include a provision imposing addi-tional duties on dumped goods in the Underwood Tariff Act of 1913.[b]

Because this provision was deleted, the Republicans continued their quest for a tarrifflike antidumping statute during the war years, claiming that predatory dumping was a frequent past and present practice of the

[b] As mentioned in Chapter 3, at this time dumping was confused with undervaluation, the fraudulent misstatement of import prices on customs declarations. The source of this confu-sion was the view that the two practices had the same impact on duty assessment and rev-enue collection. Because of this, the need to prevent customs fraud was an important issue in the case for including an antidumping provision in the Underwood Tariff Act; see, e.g., U.S., Congress, House, Committee on Ways and Means, *Tariff Hearings, Undervaluation and Antidumping Duties, Hearings Before a Subcommittee of the House Committee on Ways and Means,* 62d Cong., 3d sess., 1913, pp. 6149–50.

Moreover, the confusion of dumping with undervaluation appears to have been present when the United States Antidumping Act was initially formalized; see U.S., Congress, House, Committee on Ways and Means, *Antidumping and Undervaluation Hearings, Hear-ings Before a Subcommittee of the House Committee on Ways and Means,* 66th Cong., 1st sess., 1919, p. 5.

European nations. President Wilson opposed high tariffs, however, and wanted any antidumping legislation divorced from ordinary customs laws so that it would not yield a generally protective increase in import duties. Consequently, to alleviate protectionist pressure for customs levies to penalize dumping, he included a criminal provision against the practice in the Revenue Act of 1916.[37] This provision proved to be unenforceable because its application required proof of intent to injure competition on the part of the importer; and, the Republicans therefore renewed their antidumping effort in 1919 with a bill introduced by Congressman Fordney.[c]

From 1919 to late April 1921, the Republican attempt to pass Congressman Fordney's bill was kept alive by the widespread belief that Europe was currently dumping large quantities of goods in the United States in order to destroy American industries.[38] In late April, testimony before the Senate Finance Committee revealed that, in fact, no dumping was taking place in 1921, nor had there been any since the war. To the contrary, the experts testified that Europe was destitute and thus in no position to dump. Moreover, American prices were the highest in the world and, consequently, there was no reason for foreign concerns to dump even if they wished to invade American markets.[39] This knowledge did not prevent the passage of the Antidumping Act in May, however, for the Republicans had gained control of Congress and the executive in the election of 1920; and, regardless of the true state of world trade, they continued to favor erecting customs barriers to ensure industrial prosperity.

In an immediate sense, then, a transitory belief in the presence of dumping and the election of a protectionist Congress were of overriding importance to the birth of the Antidumping Act. More fundamentally, behind these phenomena lay an intense concern over the impact of the renewal of trade with Europe. The presumption was that the reestablishment of economic relations would usher in a period of fierce competition in the American marketplace; and Americans feared that the nations of Europe would resort to unfair methods of competition, including dumping, in the course of this rivalry.

The notion that the incidence of dumping would increase as trade normalized was grounded, first, in the commonly held belief that large sur-

---

[c] U.S. Congress, House, *A Bill to Provide Revenue and Encourage Domestic Industries by the Elimination, Through the Assessment of Special Duties, of Unfair Competition, and for Other Purposes,* H.R. 10918, 66th Cong., 2d sess., 1919.

This bill was ressurrected in 1921 and introduced as Title II of the Emergency Tariff Act. After being significantly altered by the Senate, Title II became the Antidumping Act of 1921. U.S., Congress, House, *A Bill Imposing Temporary Duties on Certain Agricultural Products to Meet Present Emergencies, and to Provide Revenue; to Regulate Commerce with Foreign Countries; to Prevent Dumping of Foreign Merchandise on the Markets of the United States; to Regulate the Value of Foreign Money; and for Other Purposes,* H.R. 2435, 67th Cong., 1st sess., 1921, Title II.

pluses of goods have accumulated in foreign manufacturing nations because of the suspension of trade during the war years. Allegedly, these surpluses were destined to be dumped in the United States upon the cessation of hostilities.[40] Second, the revival of the European economy would apparently require a demand for goods and services that the impoverished European consumer could not provide. Thus, there existed the possibility that Europe would throw upon the American market, at any price, output in excess of home demand to promote industrial recovery. Finally, since the main competition in American markets before the war had come from Europe, the absence of European imports had been of great significance to American industry. It had permitted American producers to expand and, more importantly, to diversify, establishing production in lines of manufacture where they previously could not compete with their European rivals. Consequently, Americans were concerned that European manufacturers would engage in predatory dumping to destroy America's numerous war-born industries and recapture their lost export markets.[41]

With respect to the "dumping" of surplus goods, during the war the United States had sold supplies to her European Allies at low prices, and Americans feared that the stocks remaining at war's end would be disposed of in the United States at prices below their cost of production. In addition, while the American airplane industry had halted production after the war, Great Britain's had not. Consequently, American producers were concerned that the British had accumulated surplus airplanes which they would endeavor to sell in the United States. In fact, rumors were adrift in 1921 that the dumping of a considerable volume of excess trucks, airplanes, and airplane engines had already begun. Although such claims eventually proved to be groundless, they furnished some support for anti-dumping legislation to prevent the disposal of surplus war material by America's Allies.[42] Of far greater concern to Americans, however, was the claim that Germany had purposefully built up inventories to be dumped after the war in order to destroy the economies of her erstwhile enemies.[43] This claim, which again proved ephemeral, had considerable emotional appeal; for, allegedly, it was in this manner that the Germans planned to gain in peacetime what had been lost during the conflagration.

Moreover, the specter of German price cutting also caused the greatest alarm about dumping to rekindle the national economy and to regain lost export markets. As mentioned above, Germany had been one of the two major dumping nations before the war—the other being the United States. Although Germany had not dumped to monopolize foreign markets except in rare instances, extensive wartime propaganda portrayed the enemy as lacking moral integrity, and, by war's end, Americans believed that Germany's prewar dumping had been predatory in the main and had injured numerous domestic industries. In general, they believed that Germany's phenomenal prewar success in international trade had been due to her willingness to employ devious and underhanded methods of competition rather than to her technological efficiency and innovative marketing, as was really the case. Furthermore, most of America's important war-born industries—such as chemical, laboratory, and optical glass: cutlery; delicate surgical instruments; and chemicals—had displaced German imports in the domestic marketplace.[44] Thus, Americans felt that Germany was most likely to dump in the postwar years because she had a record of customarily engaging in unfair trade practices, had often dumped predatorily in the past, and presently had the greatest incentive to do so.

In addition, Americans were not equally apprehensive about the threat of German dumping to each of America's infant industries. Rather, both in and out of Congress, concern over the prospect of German dumping was focused on the need to protect the neophyte American color-dye industry.

Before the war, Germany had a monopoly in many branches of the chemical industry. These monopolies were especially important because they produced goods that were inputs into more-advanced-stage industries, and thus they gave Germany control of other industries as well. An important instance of such German control occurred in the line of coal-tar color dyes, which are produced from intermediates. Because of her technical proficiency at producing color-dye intermediates and her superior business organizations, Germany had monopolized intermediates production before 1914 and directly produced three-fourths of the world's dyestuff output. In addition, she controlled half of the dye-making capacity of other countries and could influence the remainder of foreign production through her monopoly of intermediates.[45] Moreover, the German dye combines emerged from the war with their organizations and productive facilities intact.

On the other hand, the American chemical industry was insignificant in size before the war. In the field of dyestuffs, America produced only 10% of her needs and even this production was dependent on German inputs. During the war, however, American production expanded sharply as a result of the curtailment of German imports and the war demand.[46] At war's end, the capacity to produce color dyes exceeded peacetime needs; and hence, in the advent of free trade and a concerted German effort to reestablish her supremacy, there was good reason to fear that American dye manufacturers would not survive.

In an effort to insulate itself from German competition after the war, the American dye industry expended most of its energy in backing the Chemical Control Act of 1921, which placed an embargo on the importation of dyestuffs.[47] At the same time, antidumping legislation was viewed as a vehicle for acquiring protection, and, thus, arguments involving each of the issues mentioned above were advanced by dye-industry spokesmen during the congressional hearings and debates on the Antidumping Act.[48] In addition, they offered a new and formidable reason for protecting the dye industry from German dumping: a contention known as the "key industry" argument.

In this regard, the war had impressed upon the world the relationship between a nation's ability to produce and its ability to engage in combat. Certain key industries were recognized as essential to warmaking, and, with the strong nationalist sentiment that followed the war, it was felt that a nation should cultivate and maintain these industries at all costs. Surprisingly, the color-dye industry emerged during the war as a key industry because, with only a slight alteration, the dyemaking process can be used to produce picric acid. Picric acid in turn is a shell filler for which there was great demand during the war because toluol, the best explosive for filling shells, was in short supply.[49]

Thus, it turned out that the color-dye industry was of great military importance, and after the war some legislators argued that Germany had secretly monopolized dye production to prepare for world conquest. She had done so, they claimed, through dumping and other illicit practices, and she was likely to use these methods to attempt to do so again. Consequently, during the period in which the dye embargo was uncertain of passage, the industry's spokesmen defended the Antidumping Act as necessary to the future of peace.[50]

Although the main effort of the dye industry was not spent in lobbying the Antidumping Act, the dye-industry issue injected an important new element into America's concern about dumping, since it made the prospect of postwar dumping more than a general threat to industrial prosperity. At least in the case of the dye industry, dumping was a serious threat to a key industry and to America's military security.

Finally, no discussion of the postwar conditions amenable to the enactment of antidumping legislation would be complete without the observation that the Antidumping Act was a natural adjunct to the type of commercial policy that the Republicans advocated during the postwar period. Having suffered through seven years of low tariff rates contained in the Underwood Tariff, the Republicans were determined to pass a tariff increase of more or less general scope. The purpose of this increase was to set business on an "equal footing" with foreign competition, and thus the tariff rates were to be equal to the difference between domestic and foreign costs of production. Constructing tariffs in this manner was known as "scientific tariff making"; and the idea of a scientific tariff aimed tariff—aimed solely at protecting American industry from low-cost foreign competition and no more—was one for which protectionists had considerable zeal during this period.[51]

Dumping may be used to absorb an import duty and offset its effect on sales in the protected market. Consequently, high tariffs increase the incentive to dump. This is not likely to greatly upset the tariff maker if his purpose is to raise revenue, as had ostensibly been the aim of American tariffs in the 1800s. Tariff revenue will be less because of the lower import prices but greater because of the larger volume of imports. Dumping runs directly counter to the intent of a scientific tariff maker, however, for it erases any tariff compensation for cost differences. In effect, it puts business back on an unequal footing. Thus, the case for antidumping legislation is strengthened when one intends to pass a scientific tariff, for an antidumping act is needed as a counterpart to import duties to prevent foreign competitors from pricing so as to defeat the tariff's purpose.

## Summary and Conclusions

Although dumping is broadly defined as price discrimination in international trade, the term is most commonly used to denote price discrimination between home and foreign markets when the lower price is charged abroad. The prerequisites of the practice are a monopolistic control of home-market prices and protective tariffs; because these conditions arose between 1870 and World War I, dumping, unaccompanied by governmental export bounties, emerged as a common pricing policy. Nevertheless, dumping was not generally done to monopolize foreign markets during this period, and, as a result, little antidumping legislation was passed prior to the war.

Immediately after the war, however, many nations passed antidumping acts, including the United States. The stated purpose of the United States act was to prevent the monopolization of domestic markets; however, the history of dumping and early antidumping laws suggests that the Act was not a response to a frequent experience with the anticompetitive effects of foreign dumping. Rather, it appears to owe its origin to economic and political conditions peculiar to the postwar years.

In this regard, it is instructive to note that, during this period, many domestic industries were weak and their futures uncertain. The revival of trade threatened the continued existence of these war-born industries and augured a general intensification of distrust among nations. America harbored an isolationist sentiment. There was a renaissance in protectionism; and protectionists were advocating a scientific tariff to which antidumping legislation was a natural counterpart. Thus, the Antidumping Act was the product of an era in which economic and political conditions were radically different from the present circumstances of established patterns of industrial development, continuing international trade, recognized interdependence between nations, and an ongoing process of trade liberalization.

In addition, to a significant degree, the Antidumping Act was founded on fantasy. At the Act's inception, the term "dumping" was still subject to misconstruction. Throughout most of its journey through Congress, the Act was accompanied by the irrational belief that dumping was currently rampant and that Europe had accumulated enormous surpluses that would eventually be dumped in the United States. Moreover, wartime propaganda had resulted in the unfounded opinion that Germany had frequently practiced predatory dumping. By dividing the world into good guys—who dumped only to minimize costs—and bad guys—who had a history of dumping to monopolize—wartime propaganda permitted the passage of an antidumping act aimed at controlling the actions of foreign monopolists exporting to the United States only three years after the Webb-Pomerene Act had exempted American producers from the purview of the Sherman Act in their international dealings.

Furthermore, at the inception of the Act, the economics of dumping was little understood. The works of Viner, on dumping proper, and Robinson, on the general problem of price discrimination were still to come. Yet each of these works provides grounds for questioning the content of the law: Viner's, because it offers an argument for preventing dumping aside from its predatory potential; Robinson's, because it demonstrates that dumping is less likely to be predatory and more likely to result in continuously low import prices than previously thought. In light of these and other significant writings since 1921, it is apparent that Congress lacked a substantial and pertinent body of information on dumping at the time that it considered the Antidumping Act. And yet, the Act has not been amended to reflect this new knowledge.

The Antidumping Act represented a radical departure from previous congressional policy. Whereas Congress had hitherto jealously guarded its tax and tariff-making powers, in the Antidumping Act it delegated quasi-tariff-making power to the executive. It permitted the Secretary of the Treasury to decide how intensively to investigate a given claim of dumping. Within certain limits, it allowed him to exercise his judgment in calculating whether dumping had occurred. It left to the Secretary, and later, the International Trade Commission, responsibility for defining the meaning of "injury to an American industry" in determining if an instance of dumping endangered competition in a domestic market. And, ultimately, it empowered the Secretary to levy additional duties on imports whenever injurious dumping was found. Thus, either because it was protectionist or because it was influenced by the pleas of businessmen to protect their interests, a future administration could use the Act to unfairly limit importation.

While United States commercial policy has evolved from protectionism to trade liberalization, the Antidumping Act has not changed signifi-·cantly since 1921. It stands today as a potentially protectionist statute in an era of falling tariffs and trade barriers. Consequently, it is not surprising that in the last decade lawyers and economists have expressed reservations about the merits of the law. Lawyers have debated whether the responsible agencies have given the Act a "tariff" or an "antitrust" interpretation. Economists have voiced the fear that the Act may be increasingly relied on as a nontariff barrier to trade as tariffs disappear. Both groups have raised the more general issue of the proper application of the Act in the light of America's current liberal trade policy and the international standards of the GATT Code.

In view of the origin and nature of the Antidumping Act, policymakers are rightfully concerned with each of these issues today. Perhaps they can all be clarified if we inspect the current state of economic theory pertaining to dumping and deduce some conclusions as to how dumping ought to be regulated, so as to maximize welfare. In the next chapter, this task is begun by considering the impact of dumping on the welfare of exporting nations and the rationality of America's failure to regulate dumping by its exporters.

## Endnotes

1. *Antidumping Act, U.S. Code,* vol. 19, secs. 160–73 (1970).

2. Ibid., sec. 160(a).

3. Contracting Parties to the General Agreement on Tariffs and Trade, *Agreement on the Implementation of Article VI (Antidumping Code)* (Geneva: General Agreement on Tariffs and Trade, 1969).

4. Jacob Viner, *Dumping: A Problem in International Trade* (Chicago: University of Chicago Press, 1923, reprinted 1966, A. M. Kelly Publishing, New York), pp. 3–5. © 1923 by the University of Chicago Press. Reprinted by permission.

5. See Roger Q. Miles, "Tariff Issues Plainly Stated," in *Readings in the Economic and Social History of the United States,* eds. Felix Flugel and Harold U. Faulkner (New York: Harper Bros. Publishers, 1929), p. 536.

6. See William Harbutt Dawson, *The Evolution of Modern Germany* (New York: C. Schribner's Sons, 1914), pp. 179–81.

7. Viner, p. 6.

8. O. P. Austin, *Economics of World Trade* (New York: Business Training Corp., 1916), pp. 53–57.

9. U.S., Congress, House, *Emergency Tariff Bill,* H. Rept. 1 to Accompany H.R. 2435, 67th Cong., 1st sess., 1921, pp. 3–5.

10. U.S., Congress, Senate, 67th Cong., 1st sess., 6 May 1921, *Congressional Record* 61:1099.

11. H. W. de Jonge, "The Significance of Dumping in International Trade," *Journal of World Trade Law* 2 (1968):162–65. In the 1920s and 1930s some governments did enact legislation to prevent "social dumping;" see U.S., Cong., Senate, *Antidumping Legislation and Other Import Regulations in the United States and Foreign Countries,* S. Doc. 112, 73d Cong., 2d sess., 1934, pp. 13–14.

12. U.S., Congress, House, 74th Cong., 2d sess., 22 August 1935, *Congressional Record* 79:14124–25.

13. Viner, pp. 15–16.

14. U.S., Congress, House, *A Bill Imposing Temporary Duties on Certain Agricultural Products to Meet Present Emergencies, and to Provide Revenue; to Regulate Commerce with Foreign Countries; to Prevent Dumping of Foreign Merchandise on the Markets of the United States; to Regulate the Value of Foreign Money; and for Other Purposes,* H.R. 2435, 67th Cong., 1st sess., 1921, Title II, sec. 214.

15. See John Day Larkin, *The President's Control of the Tariff* (Cambridge: Harvard University Press, 1936), pp. 175–76; and Viner, pp. 163–64.

16. See J. Wilczynski, "Dumping and Central Planning," *Journal of Political Economy* 74 (June 1966): 250–65; and F. D. Holzman, "Some Financial Aspects of Soviet Foreign Trade," in *Comparisons of United States and Soviet Economies,* U.S., Congress, Joint Economic Committee (Washington, D.C.: Government Printing Office, 1959), pt. 2, pp. 429–33.

17. F. W. Taussig, *Some Aspects of the Tariff Question,* 3d ed. (Cambridge: Harvard University Press, 1931), pp. 208–10.

18. Viner, p. 84.

19. Ibid., pp. 94–95.

20. Gottfried von Haberler, *The Theory of International Trade* (London: William Hodge and Co., Ltd., 1936), p. 301.

21. William Arthur Seavy, *Dumping since the War; The GATT and National Laws* (Oakland: Office Services Corp., 1970), pp. 2–5.

22. Viner, p. 23.

23. Milton Gilbert, "A Sample Study of Differences Between Domestic and Export Pricing Policies of United States Corporations," in *Investigation of Concentration of Economic Power,* U.S., Congress, Senate, Temporary National Economic Committee (Washington, D.C.: Government Printing Office, 1941), monograph no. 6, pp. 3–93. For a criticism of Gilbert's work see John Scoville and Noel Sargent, *Facts and Fancy in the TNEC Monographs* (New York: National Association of Manufacturers, 1942), pp. 77–78.

24. Ibid., pp. 91–93.

25. Ibid., pp. 82–83.

26. See Edward Chamberlin, *The Theory of Monopolistic Competition,* 8th ed. (Cambridge: Harvard University Press, 1962); and Joan Robinson, *The Economics of Imperfect Competition* (London: Macmillan and Co., Ltd., 1933), bk. 5.

27. "Trusts and Protection," *Protectionist* 16 (November 1904):361–62.

28. U.S., Congress, Senate, Statement and Exhibits Submitted by Senator Humphrey Concerning the Recent Dumping of Steel, 88th Cong., 1st sess., 27 May 1963, *Congressional Record* 109:9536–39.

29. Y. R. Maroni, "Discrimination under Market Interdependence," *Quarterly Journal of Economics* 62 (November 1947):101–6.

30. Unless otherwise footnoted, all material in this section pertaining to dumping is drawn from Viner, chaps. 3–5.

31. Larkin, pp. 172–74.

32. See also, Larkin, pp. 153–56.

33. Herbert Heaton, *Economic History of Europe,* rev. ed. (New York: Harper and Row, Publishers, 1948), pp. 638–48.

34. See Dawson, pp. 172–75; Heaton, p. 605; and George W. Stocking and Myron W. Watkins, *Cartels or Competition?* (New York: Twentieth Century Fund, 1948), p. 29.

35. U.S., Congress, Senate, *Antidumping Legislation and Other Import Regulations in the United States and Foreign Countries,* pp. 29–65.

36. Ibid.

37. Viner, pp. 242–43.

38. See U.S., Congress, House, *Emergency Tariff Bill,* p. 23; and U.S., Congress, Senate, 67th Cong., 1st sess., 6 May 1921, *Congressional Record* 61:1099, 1103–4.

39. U.S., Congress, Senate, Committee on Finance, *Emergency Tariff and Antidumping, Hearings Before a Subcommittee of the Senate Committee on Finance on H.R. 2435,* 67th Cong., 1st sess., 1921, pp. 36–38, 60–61, 90–101.

40. U.S., Congress, Senate, *Duties on Imports,* S. Rept. 510 to Accompany H.R. 10918, 66th Cong., 2d sess., 1920, pt. 2.

41. William Smith Culbertson, *Commercial Policy in Wartime and After* (New York: D. Appleton and Co., 1919), pp. 149–50.

42. U.S., Congress, Senate, 66th Cong., 2d sess., 17 April 1920, *Congressional Record* 59:5769; U.S., Congress, Senate, 67th Cong., 1st sess., 6 May 1921, *Congressional Record* 61:1099; and U.S., Congress, Senate, 67th Cong., 1st sess., 10 May 1921, *Congressional Record* 61:1292–93.

43. See U.S., Congress, Senate, Committee on Finance, *Emergency Tariff and Antidumping Hearings,* p. 125.

44. Culbertson, pp. 20–62.

45. Ibid., pp. 33–35.

46. See Culbertson, pp. 33–61; with respect to the dye industry, U.S., Congress, Senate, Committee on Finance, *Tariff Act of 1921, Dye Embargo, Hearings Before a Subcommittee of the Senate Committee on Finance on H.R. 7456,* 67th Cong., 1st sess., 1921, pp. 436–37.

47. U.S., Congress, Senate, Committee on Finance, *Tariff Act of 1921, Dye Embargo Hearings,* passim.

48. U.S., Congress, House, Committee on Ways and Means, *Antidumping and Undervaluation Hearings, Hearings Before a Subcommittee of the House Committee on Ways and Means,* 66th Cong., 1st sess., 1919, pp. 13–14; U.S., Congress, House, 66th Cong., 2d sess., 9 December 1919, *Congressional Record* 59:327–32; and U.S., Congress, Senate, Committee on Finance, *Emergency Tariff and Antidumping Hearings,* p. 125.

49. Culbertson, pp. 52–58.

50. U.S., Congress, Senate, Senator Knox speaking in favor of the embargo on dyestuffs, 67th Cong., 1st sess., 9 May 1921, *Congressional Record* 61:1190–91; see also Percy Wells Bidwell, *What the Tariff Means to American Industries* (New York: Harper and Co., 1956), p. 188.

51. Felix Flugel and Harold U. Faulkner, eds., *Readings in the Economic and Social History of the United States* (New York: Harper Bros. Publishers, 1929), p. 487; see also, Culbertson, p. 137 et seq.

# 2

# The Effect of Dumping on Welfare in the Exporting Nation

In the preceding chapter, it was observed that consumers in the exporting country have often complained of dumping because they pay a higher price than foreign purchasers. Similarly, advanced-stage industries have objected to the dumping of raw materials, claiming that the price disparity puts them at a competitive disadvantage vis-a-vis foreign fabricators both in their home market and in markets abroad. Nevertheless, nations have not attempted to regulate export dumping in the interest of enhancing domestic welfare. And, in fact, a proposal tendered by New Zealand in 1955 which required nations to prevent dumping by their producers was rejected by the contracting parties to the GATT.[a] With respect to the absence of controls on export dumping in the United States statutes, in 1919 Congressman Fordney stated that the maintenance of high domestic prices was necessary to ensure the profitability of American business, while the dumping of surplus production abroad was necessary to sustain employment and reduce costs. Consequently, Mr. Fordney felt that the United States should not try to control export prices because such controls could only redound to the detriment of Americans.[1]

The effect of dumping on welfare in the exporting nation, however, is by no means as clear-cut and salubrious as Mr. Fordney suggested. And in view of the complaints that have been lodged, a question arises as to whether the lack of concern about export dumping in the United States Antidumping Act reflects a proindustry bias on the part of its founders, a technical inability to legislate against the practice, or the absence of a detriment to the exporting society from such pricing behavior. Consequently, in this chapter, the effect of dumping on welfare in the exporting country is analyzed. The chapter begins with a review of the work of other economists which summarizes the diversity of opinion on the subject. In the next four sections, the welfare effect of dumping is appraised with great reliance on the writings of J. Robinson and Y. O. Yntema. In the conclusion, an answer is provided to the question, is the absence of controls on export dumping justified by welfare considerations?

---

[a] The members of the GATT, however, did adopt a proposal recommending that participant nations "refrain from encouraging dumping" by their industries; see John H. Jackson, *World Trade and the Law of GATT* (New York: Bobbs-Merrill Co., Inc., 1969), p. 412, nn. 9, 10.

## Evolution of the Subject

Economists have always maintained that dumping must increase the profits of the dumper since he invariably retains the option of charging identical prices in all markets. They have reasoned, nevertheless, that dumping may decrease welfare in the exporting country, for the overall welfare effect of dumping also depends on its impact on other economic actors and on the general state of the economy. The side effects customarily examined in assessing the total welfare effect of dumping in the exporting nation have been its impact on consumers and fabricating industries, the distribution of income, and the balance of payments. Of these side effects, the ramification of dumping for consumer welfare and the competitive viability of second-stage industries have been by far the most important considerations: the usual analysis balancing the gain to the exporter against any loss to domestic users of the dumped goods.

Before modern economic analysis was applied to the problem of price discrimination, economists held varying opinions about the effect of dumping on consumers and processing industries in the home country. J. A. Schumpeter wrote that dumping involves the foreign sale of goods which would have been sold at home and that, consequently, under dumping, domestic prices will be higher than otherwise. Hence, dumping imposes a burden on domestic purchasers.[2] On the other hand, Jacob Viner felt that dumping never changes the monopolist's profit-maximizing home price, nor does it normally lower foreign prices since price cutting is only advantageous to the predator. He concluded, optimistically, that dumping does not affect the home consumer vis-a-vis foreign rivals.[3] However, the prevailing view, according to Gottfried von Haberler, was that dumping enables the cartel to decrease costs by producing a larger output, and thus causes domestic prices to fall.[4] In spite of the diversity of opinion, the general belief was that dumping benefitted domestic users as well as increasing the profits of the dumper and, consequently, that dumping was advantageous to the exporting nation.

In 1928 Yntema applied the tools of demand and supply analysis to the problem of dumping under a limited set of economic conditions.[5] Five years later, Robinson published her seminal work on the general problem of price discrimination, which involved a marginalist analysis of price discrimination under more varied circumstances than those encompassed by Yntema's inquiry.[6] The primary objective of these discussions was to disclose how the substitution of price discrimination for single pricing affects the firm's total output and the level of prices and sales in the markets involved.[7] With respect to the phenomenon of dumping, the studies revealed that the effect of dumping on the home price and, thus, its welfare consequences in the exporting country depends heavily upon the economic conditions in which the dumping occurs. Without a specification of the milieu in which dumping takes place, one cannot tell whether the practice will be beneficial or detrimental to domestic consumers or, on balance, to the exporting society.

A third important contribution was offered by S. Enke in 1946.[8] Writing on monopoly in trade, Enke recommended that in order to maximize domestic welfare governments should require exporters to equate home price to foreign marginal revenue to marginal cost in choosing their output level and dividing sales between home and foreign markets. The second of Enke's optimality conditions follows from the marginalist maxim that production should be extended until marginal benefits equal marginal opportunity cost, and it amounts to the preclusion of monopoly pricing at home. The first condition arises from the observation that domestic welfare will only be maximized if the last unit of a good exported earns a value of imports equal to the utility value that consumers would have received had the article been sold domestically. Thus, welfare cannot be maximized as long as exporters dump, since, under dumping, foreign marginal revenue is less than the price charged in domestic markets. Accordingly, in Enke's view, dumping should be forbidden, and firms should be forced to reverse dump when the foreign market is not perfectly competitive and price singly in all markets when it is.[9]

The question of the effect of dumping on welfare in the exporting country has not been widely discussed in recent articles on the subjects of international price discrimination and antidumping laws. When the topic has appeared, the authors have not inspected Robinson's theory of price discrimination, nor have they provided a dichotomized treatment of the welfare effects of dumping leading to conditional conclusions. Rather, they have indulged in brief, general appraisals of whether dumping is salutary to domestic welfare, overall.

W. A. Seavy, for example, reiterates Yntema's conclusion that the effect of dumping on consumers in the home country varies with the shape of the dumper's cost curves. Seavy observes that the dumper must obtain higher profits, while advanced-stage industries are likely to be hurt by the dumping of inputs; and given this hodgepodge of effects, he decides to abstain from judging the value of the practice to the exporting nation.[10]

On the other hand, H. W. de Jonge (1968) and B. S. Fisher (1973) combine the conclusions of Enke, Robinson, and Yntema to produce eclectic discussions that proceed first in the direction of neutrality only to arrive at negative pronouncements.[11] Like Seavy, these authors begin by summarily accounting for the effects of dumping on particular groups. They note that the exporter's profits are sure to climb, that fabricating industries will be disadvantaged, and that consumers may gain or lose according as dumping raises or lowers the home price. They speculate that dumping may have value as a temporary palliative to a balance-of-payments deficit, but that it is not a constructive way to alleviate unemployment because it puts workers to inefficient use. Given this mixture of positive and negative effects, it may appear that Seavy was right: that the welfare consequences of dumping for the home country are too uncertain to be judged. However, this position is unfounded; to quote Fisher:

There is, in any case, a misallocation of resources in the exporting country when intermittent or continuous dumping takes place. Such dumping cannot be successful without the artificial conditions of barriers to reentry into the domestic market and some monopolistic control of the home market. These facts, as de Jonge notes, 'condemn the existing economic situation in the exporting country as an inefficient one, because of the misallocation of its productive resources. This country could raise its economic welfare by reducing the output of the dumped article, stop dumping abroad, and expand production of something else.'[12]

Thus, de Jonge and Fisher escape from the ambiguities that arise because dumping is beneficial in some ways and detrimental in others by conjuring up an argument that looks suspiciously like Enke's; and therein lies their error. For Enke did not show that for the exporting country dumping was an inferior policy compared to single pricing. He showed that monopoly pricing at home accompanied by dumping was an inferior policy to competitive pricing domestically and single pricing or reverse dumping in trade. His policy recommendation was simultaneously to prevent dumping and, importantly, monopoly pricing upon the home market. Yet, de Jonge and Fisher were addressing the issue of whether dumping itself benefits the exporting country as compared to single pricing, with no change in the firm's domestic monopoly position. Their policy recommendation is only to preclude dumping itself as a pernicious phenomenon.

In reality, however, the misallocation of resources of which de Jonge and Fisher speak is not created by the act of dumping but by the existence of monopoly. And it cannot be cured by desisting from dumping, but only through the elimination of monopoly. In fact, to follow their remedy would necessarily lower domestic welfare; for the profit-maximizing dumper sells at home and abroad so as to equate domestic marginal revenue to foreign marginal revenue to marginal cost. Thus, "to reduce the production of the dumped article, stop dumping abroad, and expand production of something else" would involve sacrificing exports for which the value of freed resources in other-goods production is less than their value in earning foreign exchange.

It is, then, hard to get away from the ramifications of the Robinson-Yntema analysis: that dumping may be beneficial to some groups and detrimental to others, that it may benefit home consumers in one instance and hurt them in another, and, because of this, that its effect on welfare is hard to assess. Accordingly, in the following three sections, Robinson's analysis of price discrimination is used to describe the economic conditions under which dumping will raise welfare in the exporting country, the circumstances in which it will lower welfare, and the circumstances in which it may do either. Subsequently, the assumptions underlying this discussion are dropped, and the effect of their absence on our conclusions is investigated.

**Analytical Framework**

In the introduction of this chapter, it was indicated that the traditional way of analyzing the effect of dumping on welfare in the home country was, first, to observe that dumping increases the producer's profits and, subsequently, to assess its effect on consumers and processing industries. The central issue was whether or not the latter two groups experience any decrease in welfare because of the dumping and, if so, whether the negative impact that they experience is great enough to offset the benefit of increased profitability. Both the effect of dumping on the dumper's net revenue and on consumers and advanced-stage-industry welfare are, in general terms, the outcome of a redistribution of resources between industries which dumping causes. In the section below, we shall examine the change in welfare that occurs because dumping results in a reallocation of resources within the exporting economy. Our analysis will thus encompass the effects of dumping on consumers, other producers, and the exporter that traditionally have been inspected, although we will not be particularly concerned with maintaining this division.

In order to simplify the analysis, our inspection will be conducted under the following assumptions:

1. Full employment exists in the exporting country;
2. All markets are perfectly competitive except the product market of the dumping industry;
3. The dumper does not have to raise factor prices in order to acquire additional resources;
4. The dumper produces a final-consumption good;
5. Whether dumping or single pricing, the firm's profit function has only one local maximum;
6. The dumping margin is not limited by incomplete market separation;
7. The firm's only goal is to maximize profits;
8. Any changes in production, home and foreign sales, or income due to dumping are too small to change the marginal utility of money or shift demand curves;
9. At a given price, demand is less elastic at home than abroad;
10. Like the corresponding demand curves, both the home and foreign marginal revenue curves are continuously downward sloping.

Assumptions 1, 2, and 3 are made to facilitate a discussion of welfare changes by assuring that the maximum demand price of any $i$th unit of production is its welfare value to consumers while the marginal cost of producing the unit is its social opportunity cost. Assumptions 4, 5, and 6 are made to rule out certain anomalous results discussed by other authors which will be accounted for when the assumptions are dropped. Assumption 8 permits us to engage in partial-equilibrium analysis, and assumptions 9 and 10 ensure that the firm will dump, and not reverse dump, when allowed to price discriminate.

Furthermore, since economic conditions importantly influence the impact of dumping on the allocation of resources and the distribution of sales between markets, we will eventually divide our analysis according to some additional assumptions about the circumstances in which dumping takes place. Before entering into the analysis of dumping under specific sets of conditions, however, let us examine the general impact of dumping on output and describe the implications of different changes in resource use and sales mix for welfare in the home country.

### Relationship Between Changes in Output and Changes in Welfare

A profit-maximizing producer may choose not to engage in trade if he must set equal prices in all markets but may be willing to export if permitted to dump. In this instance, he will maximize profits by producing and selling at home a volume of goods that equates marginal cost ($MC$) to domestic marginal revenue ($MR_h$). At the same time, it must be true that the potential marginal revenue obtainable from the first unit of exports ($MR_f$) must be less than the prevailing home price ($P_h$) and greater than the prevailing marginal revenue acquired domestically. If the latter condition did not hold, foreign marginal revenue would be less than marginal cost under profit maximization in autarky, and even the option to dump would not induce the producer to export. On the other hand, if the foreign marginal revenue obtainable from initial sales abroad exceeded the profit-maximizing home price, trade would unambiguously take place under single pricing. Thus, when a profit maximizer chooses to restrict sales to the home market under single pricing, but not under dumping, he will produce and sell output so that equation (2.1) obtains.

$$p_h > MR_f > MR_h = MC. \qquad (2.1)$$

If, instead the producer finds it profitable to engage in trade while single pricing, he must first increase domestic sales until the home price becomes equal to the maximum nonzero-demand price abroad and then divide further sales between home and foreign markets so as to maintain price equality. Consequently, once he begins exporting, his marginal revenue will be a convex linear combination of home and foreign marginal revenues with the additive coefficients equaling the percentage of the last unit of output that must be sold in each market to maintain equal prices ($\overline{MR}$). Moreover, the coefficients in the monopolist's single-price marginal revenue equation will depend only on the relative slopes of the two market demand curves. To see this, let domestic and foreign demand be expressed by $P_h = H(Q_h)$ and $P_f = F(Q_f)$. Then, to maintain equality between $P_h$ and $P_f$, it is necessary that $h' dQ_h/dQ_t = f' dQ_f/dQ_t$ with respect to the division of incremental output between markets. Since $dQ_t = dQ_h + dQ_f$, equations (2.2)–(2.4) follow:

$$h' \frac{dQ_h}{dQ_t} = f' - f' \frac{dQ_h}{dQ_t}, \tag{2.2}$$

and

$$\frac{dQ_h}{dQ_t} = \frac{f'}{f' + h'} \qquad \frac{dQ_f}{dQ_t} = \frac{h'}{f' + h'}. \tag{2.3}$$

Thus,

$$\overline{MR} = \frac{f'}{f' + h'} MR_h + \frac{h'}{f' + h'} MR_f. \tag{2.4}$$

Furthermore, since $MR = P(1 + 1/\eta)$, it follows from assumption 9 that $MR_f$ must be greater than $MR_h$ in equation (2.4). Under profit maximization while charging identical prices at home and abroad, marginal revenue, as derived above, will be set equal to marginal cost; and therefore, initially, output and sales will be such that equation (2.5) holds.

$$P_h = P_f \geq MR_f > \overline{MR} = MC > MR_h. \tag{2.5}$$

Whether or not he decides to sell abroad while single pricing, the profit maximizer will distribute his sales so that $MR_f$ exceeds $MR_h$. Consequently, the transisition from a regime of unitary pricing to one of dumping may be viewed as a two-step process. The producer first redistributes sales from the home market to the foreign market, keeping output constant, until $MR_f = MR_h$. In doing so, he increases his profits since the additional revenue gained from each new unit of export sales exceeds the revenue lost from abstaining from domestic disposal. Once this redistribution is completed, the two marginal revenues may be greater than, equal to, or less than marginal cost, which has not changed. Thus, the firm will subsequently adjust total output until marginal revenue in each market equals marginal cost. Since $MR_h = MR_f$ at the beginning of this second step, sales in both markets will move in the same direction as output: expanding if the profit-maximizing strategy calls for an increase in production and contracting if profit maximization calls for a decrease. In either case, changes in sales in the two markets will be made in such proportions as to maintain the equality of marginal revenues.

If there is no exportation before the advent of dumping, dumping must lead to an increase in output and sales since initially $MR_f > MR_h = MC$, and the redistributive step by which the two marginal revenues are equated must leave them above marginal cost in production. Thus, the effect of the output-adjustment step will necessarily be to reinforce the tendency for exports to rise and to partially or totally reverse the previous fall in home sales.

However, if the firm engages in trade under single pricing, the direction of the change in total output that dumping will generate depends on the shape of the demand curves in the home and foreign markets. From equation (2.4) we can deduce that the ratio of the excess of foreign marginal revenue over the single-pricer's weighted-average marginal revenue to the deficit of domestic marginal revenue below this average equals the ratio of the slopes of the respective demand curves, as shown in equations (2.6) and (2.7).

$$\overline{MR} = \frac{f'}{f' + h'} MR_h + \frac{h'}{f' + h'} MR_f$$

$$O = \frac{f'}{f' + h'}(MR_h - \overline{MR}) + \frac{h'}{f' + h'}(MR_f - \overline{MR}). \qquad (2.6)$$

Therefore

$$\frac{MR_f - \overline{MR}}{\overline{MR} - MR_h} = \frac{f'}{h'}. \qquad (2.7)$$

Now, let $h_r$ and $f_r$ equal the slopes of the home and foreign marginal revenue curves, and let $\bar{h}_r$ and $\bar{f}_r$ equal the average values of these parameters between the single-pricer's home-and-foreign-sales solution and the sales solution that obtains after the redistributive step. The parameters $h_r$ and $f_r$ tell us the change in marginal revenue in each market as units of output are transferred from home to abroad during sales redistribution. The ratio of their average values, $\bar{f}_r/\bar{h}_r$, tells us how fast foreign marginal revenue falls per dollar increase in home marginal revenue, as the firm rearranges sales so as to bring the two marginal revenues into equality. Hence, if $\bar{f}_r/\bar{h}_r = f'/h'$, redistribution will equate $MR_h$ to $MR_f$ at the value of $\overline{MR}$ in the single-price, profit-maximizing equilibrium. After redistribution, both home and foreign marginal revenue will equal marginal cost, and no change in total output will take place. On the other hand, if $\bar{f}_r/\bar{h}_r$

exceeds $f'/h'$, when the marginal revenues in the two markets are equated they will lie below $\overline{MR}$ and $MC$, and output will be reduced in the second step. Thus, generally, resort to dumping will raise or lower total output or leave it unchanged, according as the ratio of the slopes of the foreign and home demand curves in single-price equilibrium is greater than, less than, or equal to the ratio of the average slopes of the respective marginal revenue curves between single-price equilibrium and equilibrium after sales redistribution.[13] Furthermore, since $f' = \bar{f}_r = 0$ when the foreign market is perfectly competitive, dumping will not change total output when the firm exports under single pricing to competitive foreign markets.

With respect to welfare, the exchange of domestic for foreign sales that occurs during the redistributive step must lower welfare in the exporting country. The dollar value of utility of the $i$th unit of home sales to native consumers equals the maximum price that they are willing to pay and just buy the $i$th unit ($\bar{P}_h$). Thus, for each unit decline in home sales, the domestic economy loses a dollar value of satisfaction equal to the maximum demand price of that unit considered as the marginal unit; or, alternatively, the decrease in satisfaction is equivalent to the home price that prevailed when the lost unit of sales was the last unit of sales. The gain to the exporting economy is the acquisition of additional imports from abroad due to the rise in foreign sales and foreign-exchange earnings. The dollar value of utility garnered from additional importation is equal to the foreign marginal revenue acquired by selling one more unit of a good abroad. It was shown above that regardless of whether or not trade occurs under single pricing, the single-pricer's profit-maximizing, sales-and-output solution will be one in which $P_h > MR_f$. Thus, any initial unit of output transformed from home to foreign sales due to dumping will cause a decline in domestic welfare of $MR_f - \bar{P}_h$ ($<0$). Moreover, since $P_h$ will increase as home sales diminish, and since $MR_f$ will decrease or remain constant as foreign sales augment, as the redistribution of sales proceeds, the drop in welfare for each successive unit of goods sold abroad will become greater and greater. Hence, a large decrease in home sales is particularly indicative of a strongly negative welfare effect due to dumping; since in addition to the greater volume of consumption foregone, the average welfare loss per unit sales decline is greater when the fall in domestic sales is substantial.

During the subsequent adjustment of production to equate marginal revenue in the two markets to marginal cost, welfare will rise if output rises; because the dumper will only increase output if, after redistributing sales, $P_h > MR_h = MR_f > MC$. Since we have assumed both perfect competition in all other domestic markets and full employment, marginal cost represents (in money terms) the alternative welfare value of the resources needed to produce one more unit of monopoly output. Thus, to the extent that home sales rise, reversing the impact of the redistributive step, the domestic economy will gain $\bar{P}_h - MC$ on each new unit of sales. Simultaneously, for each additional unit of foreign sales created by an increase in output the exporting nation will be left better off by a factor $MR_f - MC$.

It cannot be stated unequivocally, however, that welfare will fall if the dumper decreases output. In this instance, resources are reallocated away from the dumping industry to the rest of the economy. The welfare gain from each unit decrease in the dumper's output is equivalent to the marginal production cost of that unit. With each one-unit decline in production, the dumper will reduce sales at home and abroad in such proportions as to maintain an equality of marginal revenues. By reasoning similar to that which led to equation (2.4), equations (2.8) follow:

$$\frac{dQ_h}{dQ_t} = \frac{f_r}{f_r + h_r} \qquad \frac{dQ_f}{dQ_t} = \frac{h_r}{f_r + h_r}. \qquad (2.8)$$

Consequently the welfare loss from an incremental decline in production will equal expression (2.9),

$$\frac{f_r}{f_r + h_r} \bar{P}_h + \frac{h_r}{f_r + h_r} MR_f, \qquad (2.9)$$

and, thus, the net change in welfare is shown in equations (2.10) –(2.11),

$$\Delta W = MC - \frac{f_r}{f_r + h_r} \bar{P}_h - \frac{h_r}{f_r + h_r} MR_f, \qquad (2.10)$$

or

$$\Delta W = \frac{f_r}{f_r + h_r} (MC - \bar{P}_h) + \frac{h_r}{f_r + h_r} (MC - MR_f). \qquad (2.11)$$

And so an incremental reduction in output will raise, leave unchanged, or lower welfare as shown in expression (2.12),

$$\frac{\bar{P}_h - MC}{MC - MR_f} \lessgtr \frac{h_r}{f_r}. \qquad (2.12)$$

Thus, it is possible for the initial subtraction of units of output to raise welfare if the home price lies sufficiently close to marginal cost after redistribution while foreign marginal revenue lies sufficiently below it. This tendency will be reinforced if $h_r$ is large relative to $f_r$ so that any reduction in output falls most heavily on foreign sales. However, as output is reduced, $MC - MR_f$ will necessarily go to zero, and, therefore, as the process of output reduction continues, incremental decreases in production must eventually have a negative impact on welfare. Given this eventuality and the fact that the redistribution of sales drives the home price upward, that is, away from marginal cost while driving foreign marginal revenue toward marginal cost, it is most probable that an adjustment of output downward will lower welfare. Any increase in welfare that does occur by this route can be assumed to be modest.

As an alternative to the above analysis, the net change in welfare that dumping causes can be associated with the final change in home sales and total output that sales redistribution and output readjustment create. If, on balance, domestic sales rise or are unchanged, total output must have risen—since the initial redistribution of sales from home to abroad must have been offset by an increase in production whose disposal was divided between the home and foreign markets. In the instance that home sales are unaltered, the situation after dumping is the same as if no redistribution had taken place, but the total expansion in output was exported until $MR_f$ became equal to $MC$. When home sales rise, the welfare effect is the same as if there was no redistribution, but output increased and was sold at home and abroad as long as $MR_h > MC$ domestically or $MR_f > MC$ in the foreign market. Thus, whenever dumping does not decrease home sales, it must increase welfare in the exporting nation.

On the other hand, if the overall effect of dumping is to lower home sales, it may increase or decrease total production, or leave it unchanged. If total production remains unchanged, the sole effect of dumping is to redistribute sales, and this must leave the exporting nation worse off than under single pricing. If production falls, the redistribution of sales is accompanied by an output adjustment that is most likely to have a further negative effect on welfare, and whose beneficial effects are likely to be moderate and too small to counterbalance the harm done by the previous sales reallocation. Thus, the overwhelming probability is that welfare will decline in this case also. Finally, if total output rises, the net change in welfare cannot be deduced with certainty. Since home sales have fallen, production will not have increased enough to offset the initial transfer of sales from domestic consumption to exportation. Thus, welfare will have declined because of an expansion of exports at the expense of a net decrease in domestic purchases. And at the same time, welfare will have increased because of an expansion of exports at the expense of the production of other goods whose value to domestic consumers was less than the value of the imports acquired through additional exportation.

## Welfare Effect of Dumping under Specific Demand and Supply Conditions

*Case I: Perfect Competition in the Foreign Market*

Ia   no trade under single pricing

Ib   trade occurs under single pricing

Within the framework developed above, let us begin our analysis by considering the case in which the foreign market is perfectly competitive. This situation is depicted in Figure 2–1, in which the meaning of the curves is as follows:

$D_h$ = the monopolist's home demand curve

$MR_h$ = the firm's home marginal revenue curve

$P_f$ = the competitive foreign price level

$MC_0$ = the firm's marginal cost curve assuming that the profit-maximizing level of home sales would fully utilize capacity

$MC_1$ = the firm's marginal cost curve assuming that excess capacity exists at the profit-maximizing level of home sales.

Figure 2–1 has been purposely drawn so as to illustrate both the case in which the domestic firm will choose to trade under single pricing and the case in which it will not. If, unlike the diagram, $P_f$ were greater than the profit-maximizing home price ($P_h$), the producer would definitely export while charging a single price. Even if he were forbidden to reverse dump at the volume of home sales at which the home and foreign price became equal, foreign marginal revenue would be greater than both home marginal revenue and marginal cost. Consequently, having equated prices, he would increase output and sell abroad until marginal cost was equated to the foreign price level.

For this reason, $P_f$ has been set lower than $P_h$ in the diagram. When this price relationship prevails, the producer must make sales at home that reduce his profits if he decides to trade. While profit-maximization in the home market requires a quantity $Q_h$, the equalization of home and foreign prices requires a volume of home sales of $Q_h'$. In order to engage in trade without dumping, the producer has to sell at home a volume of goods $Q_h' - Q_h$ on which marginal cost is greater than domestic marginal revenue and so reduce profits earned at home by the area "$G + K$." Once this has been done, however, he may sell additional output abroad as long as marginal cost is less than the foreign price, thereby garnering additional profits upon the foreign market of "$E + F$," assuming $MC_0$ to be relevant

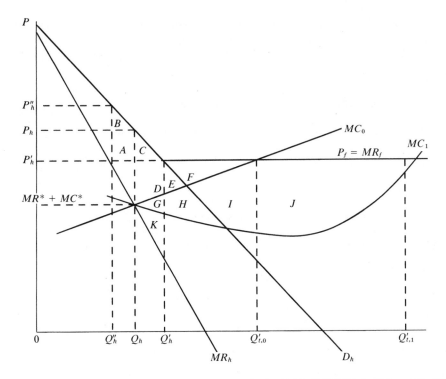

**Figure 2–1.** The Welfare Effect of Dumping in Perfectly Competitive Foreign Markets.

marginal cost curve, or "$E + F + H + I + J$" if the cost curve is $MC_1$. Consequently, the firm will trade under single pricing or will desist from exportation according as the gain in profits abroad is greater or less than the loss in profits on home sales. The firm will be more likely to trade when the foreign price is high relative to the cost structure of the firm, indicating that it has substantial comparative advantage in production over its foreign rivals, or, additionally, when profit-maximization upon the home market leaves it with significant excess capacity.

Suppose that the domestic monopolist finds it worthwhile to export even if he cannot dump. He must equate domestic and foreign prices, and thus he will dispose of $Q'_h$, domestically. He will then profit maximize by equating marginal cost to the foreign price, producing either $Q'_{t,0}$ or $Q'_{t,1}$, depending on the relevant marginal cost curve. The difference between $Q'_t$ and $Q'_h$ will, of course, be the volume of foreign sales.

The final position of the producer will thus be such that $MR_h < MR_f = MC$; and if given the option to dump, he will reallocate sales from home to abroad until the marginal revenues in the two markets are equal. As a result, domestic sales will fall from $Q'_h$ to $Q''_h$, and the home price will rise to $P''_h$.[14] Since each of the units of output between $Q'_h$ and $Q''_h$ had a welfare value in domestic consumption represented by its maximum demand price, and since each unit only earns an amount equal to the foreign price when exported, this redistribution of sales lowers welfare by area "$A + B + C$." Moreover, once the sales redistribution is accomplished, home and foreign marginal revenue will equal marginal cost, and so there will be no subsequent adjustment in total output. Hence, when the foreign market is perfectly competitive and dumping is not a prerequisite to exportation, permitting dumping will unambiguously lower welfare in the exporting nation.

On the other hand, if the producer chooses not to export under single pricing, his initial home price and quantity will be $P_h$, $Q_h$, and both domestic marginal revenue and marginal cost will lie below the foreign price. Thus, when he is permitted to dump, the producer will reduce home sales to $Q''_h$ and raise output to $Q'_{t,0}$ or to $Q'_{t-1}$ as the case may be. As explained above, the redistribution of sales away from the domestic market will lower welfare by area "$A + B$." On the other hand, the rise in output will draw resources away from the competitive sector of the economy: each unit of output having a welfare cost equivalent to its marginal cost in production and each unit furnishing a welfare gain of $P_f$. Thus, the expansion of output will raise welfare by "$D + E + F$" in the case of full capacity, or by "$D + E + F + G + H + I + J$" if there is excess capacity initially. Hence, the welfare of the exporting nation may increase or decrease depending on whether the increase in well-being due to the expansion of production counterbalances the welfare loss due to a net sales redistribution.

It is obvious from the areas of welfare gain under $MC_0$ and $MC_1$ that, when there is no trade under single pricing, dumping is more likely to raise welfare if excess capacity exists at the single-price equilibrium than if it does not. In addition, we can deduce the general impact of the shape of the home demand and marginal cost curves, and the height of foreign prices, on the net change in welfare by using equations (2.13). Let

$$P_h = a - bQ_h \qquad ATC = d + eQ_t$$

$$MR_h = a - 2bQ_h \qquad MC = d + 2eQ_t$$

$MR^*_h = MC^* =$ home marginal revenue and marginal
cost at the profit-maximizing
quantity before trade. $\qquad$ (2.13)

Since the producer will adjust home sales to equate home marginal revenue to the foreign price when he is permitted to dump, equations (2.14) must hold.

$$\Delta Q_h \frac{dMR_h}{dQ_h} = P_f - MC^*$$

$$\Delta Q_h = \frac{P_f - MC^*}{-2b}, \tag{2.14}$$

where $\Delta Q_h = Q_h'' - Q_h'$.

At the same time output will be expanded until the foreign price and marginal cost are equated, as shown in equations (2.15),

$$\Delta Q_t \frac{dMC}{dQ_t} = P_f - MC^*$$

$$\Delta Q_t = \frac{P_f - MC^*}{2e}, \tag{2.15}$$

where $\Delta Q_t = Q_{t,0} - Q_h$ or $Q_{t,1} - Q_h$.

Now, from Figure 2–1, we can observe that the total welfare change consequent upon dumping is that shown in equation (2.16),

$$\Delta W = \tfrac{1}{2} dP_h \, dQ_h + (P_h - P_f) \, dQ_h + \tfrac{1}{2} dMC \, dQ_t. \tag{2.16}$$

Substituting conditions (2.14) and (2.15) into equation (2.16), we can solve for the total change in welfare, as shown in equation (2.17),

$$\Delta W = \frac{2b - e}{8be} (P_f - MC^*)^2 - \frac{(P_h - P_f)}{2b} (P_f - MC^*). \tag{2.17}$$

Welfare will fall whenever the right-hand side of equation (2.17) is less than zero. Setting equation (2.17) less than zero, we can simplify, noting in particular that $P_h - P_f = (P_h - MC^*) - (P_f - MC^*)$. By doing so, we arrive at condition (2.18) for a fall in welfare.

$$\frac{P_f - MC^*}{P_h - MC^*} < \frac{4e}{2b + 3e} \tag{2.18}$$

Since the left-hand term must be greater than zero but less than one in the case at hand, dumping that generates exportation to perfectly competitive foreign markets will unambiguously lower welfare if the slope of the marginal cost curve is more than four times the slope of the home demand curve. Barring this restrictive condition, dumping may increase welfare, and we cannot be certain of its overall effect. Nevertheless, in the absence of excess capacity, we can state that dumping will be more likely to lower welfare the lower the foreign price is, relative to the home price and marginal cost under domestic profit maximization in autarky, the less steeply sloped is the monopolist's demand curve, and the more rapidly marginal cost rises with output.

In sum, whenever the domestic producer would choose to engage in trade under single pricing, the option to dump merely frees him to enforce a monopoly price at home in excess of world prices. For this reason, dumping must lower welfare in the exporting nation. When the producer foregoes trading under single pricing, the option to dump will similarly result in a rise in the home price, but it will also induce the producer to trade according to comparative advantage. Thus, in this instance, we cannot tell whether the institution of dumping will raise or lower social welfare. We may observe, however, that there is reason for pessimism in this matter. Those parameters of the existing economic situation which lead the single pricer to desist from exporting—a low foreign price relative to the profit-maximizing home price in autarky, a low foreign price relative to production costs, sharply increasing incremental cost, and an absence of excess capacity—are also the factors that weigh in favor of a negative welfare effect when he is permitted to dump.

*Case II: Monopoly Power in the Foreign Market: No Trade under Single Pricing*[b]

IIa   rising incremental cost
IIb   constant incremental cost
IIc   falling incremental cost

In the general discussion, it was shown that if no trade takes place under single pricing, home marginal revenue will equal marginal cost under both single pricing and dumping, in equilibrium. It was also established, in this instance, that dumping must cause production to rise. Thus, when dumping causes trade, the effect of dumping on domestic sales depends only on the shape of the firm's marginal cost curve. $MR_h$ will be greater under dumping, and domestic sales less, if marginal cost varies directly with output; the reverse result obtains if marginal cost and output vary indirectly.

In the case of perfect competition abroad, marginal cost in postdumping equilibrium had to be greater than under single pricing, because foreign marginal revenue did not fall as exportation expanded. Thus, regardless of whether costs were rising or falling in single-price equilibrium, the firm would increase production until marginal cost rose, and, in fact, until it reached a level commensurate with the foreign price, in order to profit

---

[b] The conclusions as to how dumping changes total output and home and foreign sales in this section were reached by Y. O. Yntema.

maximize. Consequently, dumping necessarily reduced domestic consumption.

The only difference between the competitive case and the present one is that when the dumper has some monopoly power abroad, both home and foreign marginal revenues fall as sales in the respective markets rise. This is an important difference, however, since it means that home and foreign marginal revenues can be equated to marginal cost at a level below that obtaining in single-price equilibrium.

Thus, if marginal cost does not vary with output, home marginal revenue will be the same in equilibrium under dumping and single pricing, and dumping will not change home sales. Its sole effect will be to permit the firm to expand output and exportation until foreign marginal revenue drops to the level of marginal cost. If marginal cost continually falls as output rises, home marginal revenue will be less under profit-maximizing dumping than under single pricing. Dumping will lead to the acquisition of foreign sales on which $MR_f$ exceeds $MC$. And it will foster an increase in home consumption which has a greater value to domestic purchasers than the alternative goods foregone. In either of these cases, dumping will increase welfare in the exporting nation, although its salutary effect will be greater when costs are falling.

On the other hand, if initially marginal cost is rising, domestic marginal revenue must be greater in postdumping equilibrium than under single pricing, and dumping will have an indeterminate welfare effect analogous to that discussed in the case of perfect competition abroad. Output and foreign sales will be greater, and this will raise welfare. But counterbalancing this, home sales will be less. Thus, when the firm refuses to export under single pricing even though it would have some control over its foreign price, dumping will benefit the exporting nation whenever marginal cost is constant or falling but may be detrimental if marginal cost is rising. Once again, when trade follows in the wake of dumping, the existence of productive capacity in excess of home demand argues in favor of dumping as in the interest of the exporting society.

*Case III:Monopoly Power in the Foreign Market:*
*Trade Occurs under Single Pricing*

IIIa output rises when dumping occurs
IIIb output falls when dumping occurs

When a firm possesses some degree of monopoly power abroad and chooses to export under single pricing, none of the conditions that simplified the analysis in the previous cases obtains. First, in the cases in which there was no exportation prior to dumping (Ib and II), we knew that profit maximization upon the home market would result in a volume of sales such that $MR_f > MR_h = MC$. Sales redistribution would leave marginal revenue in both markets above marginal cost so that dumping had to increase output. Second, it was shown earlier that when a single pricer does sell in two markets, he will equate $\overline{MR} = (f'/f' + h')MR_h + (h'/f' + h')MR_f = MC$. In the previous case of trade under single pricing and perfect competition abroad, $f'$ equaled zero and, consequently, output remained unchanged when dumping occurred. However, in the present case neither of these fortuitous conditions pertains with respect to single pricing, and so no simple prediction concerning production is possible. Rather, as has been shown above, the most we can say is that dumping will increase or decrease total output, or leave it unchanged, according as $f'/h' \gtreqqless \overline{f_r}/\overline{h_r}$.

Moreover, since, by assumption, demand is less elastic in the home market than abroad, under single pricing $MR_h$ will be less than $\overline{MR}$ and $MR_f$ will lie above it. Consequently, we cannot always predict the direction in which home and foreign sales move simply by looking at what happens to marginal cost. Occasionally, however, we will be able to resolve this dilemma by turning to our knowledge of the redistributive and output-adjustment steps that occur when price discrimination arises.

The effect of dumping on total output and home and foreign sales under conditions of monopoly abroad and trade prior to dumping is displayed in Table 2–1. The logic behind these results is as follows.

With respect to total output, our conclusion in the general analytic section showed that production will rise or fall when $\overline{MR}$ is equated to $MC$ under single pricing according as $f'/h' \gtreqqless \bar{f_r}/\bar{h_r}$, and the changes in total output are so recorded in row 1.

As to the change in domestic sales, we know, on the one hand, that when $\overline{MR} = MC$ under single pricing, $MR_h$ will be less than $MC$ and, on the other, that under dumping $MR_h$ will equal $MC$. Dumping leaves $MC$ unchanged whenever costs do not vary with output. It raises $MC$ above its level under single pricing whenever marginal cost varies directly with output and output rises under dumping, and whenever marginal cost varies inversely with output and output falls under dumping. Thus, in all of these cases (1, 2, 5, and 6), resort to dumping will lower home sales.

Marginal cost will be lower under dumping compared to single pricing whenever marginal cost varies indirectly with output and output rises, or when it varies directly with output and output falls. In the latter case (4), however, dumping must lower home sales in spite of the fact that marginal cost is lower in postdumping equilibrium; since both the redistribution of sales that occurs under dumping and any subsequent fall in output reduce home consumption. Hence, it is only in the case of a rise in output under decreasing cost conditions (3) that dumping stands to raise domestic sales. And even then—unlike the previous case of monopoly power abroad and no trade under single pricing, in which rising output and falling

**Table 2–1**

**Effect of Dumping on Total Output and Home and Foreign Sales when Trade Exists Prior to Dumping and the Firm Has Some Monopoly Power Abroad**

| $\dfrac{dMC}{dQ_t}$ | $f'/h' > \bar{f}_r/\bar{h}_r$ | | | $f'/h' < \bar{f}_r/\bar{h}_r$ | | | |
|---|---|---|---|---|---|---|---|
| | $>0$ | $=0$ | $<0$ | $>0$ | $=0$ | $<0$ | |
| $Q_t$ | + | + | + | − | − | − | (1) |
| $Q_h$ | − | − | + or − | − | − | − | (2) |
| $Q_f$ | + | + | + | + | + | + or − | (3) |
| $W$ | ? | ? | ? to + | − | − | − | (4) |
| | (1) | (2) | (3) | (4) | (5) | (6) | |

costs assured an increase in home sales—in the present case these conditions provide no guarantee.

With respect to the effect of dumping on exports, since $MR_f$ must exceed $\overline{MR}$ and $MC$ under single pricing, dumping must increase foreign sales whenever it reduces marginal cost or leaves it unchanged. Such will be the case when incremental cost does not vary with output (2 and 5), when it varies inversely with output and output rises (3), or when it varies directly with output and dumping causes production to fall (4). In the two remaining cases, exports must rise when marginal cost increases with output and output increase with dumping (1); for, although marginal cost will be greater under dumping than single pricing, both sales redistribution and output expansion cause foreign sales to rise. Since a contraction of output lowers exportation, however, when marginal cost is higher under dumping because marginal cost varies indirectly with output and output falls, foreign sales may be less than under single pricing (6).

The last row of Table 2–1 describes the net change in welfare in the exporting nation that may be associated with the changes in output and home and foreign sales listed in the columns above. Let us turn our attention first to columns (4) and (5). In each of these cases, dumping results in a net redistribution of sales away from the home market, and the welfare effect attaching to this distribution is negative. Dumping also lowers total production. Previously, we stated that a fall in production considered by itself cannot be said with certainty to lower welfare, although it is likely to do so. In the instant cases, however, it is possible to state unequivocally that the net impact of sales redistribution and output contraction, considered together, must be to lower welfare in the home country. Since foreign sales have risen on balance, the net changes in output and sales are the same as if there was, first, a redistribution of sales, having a negative impact on welfare, that raised exports to their present level; and second, a contraction of output solely involving home sales on which price exceeded marginal cost. Thus, in these cases, it can be said with certainty that domestic welfare must decline if dumping is permitted.

Similarly, with respect to column (6), if the net effect of dumping is to raise foreign sales, dumping must be harmful to social welfare. But in this instance, it is possible for foreign sales to decrease, and therefore we cannot be absolutely certain that welfare will fall upon the genesis of dumping. For while the net decline in home sales will involve a loss of marginal units of consumption on which the maximum demand price exceeds marginal cost, the net reduction in foreign sales will take place on units for which marginal cost exceeds foreign marginal revenue. Nevertheless, in spite of the resultant uncertainty as to the direction of the change in welfare, the overwhelming probability seems to be that welfare will be reduced by a policy dumping.

Finally, with respect to the cases in which dumping increases production (exhibited in the first three columns), we can conclude very little about the net change in welfare. In the case of rising or constant costs, home sales must decline if dumping is permitted, and welfare may either rise or fall. In the instance in which there is excess capacity and diminishing costs, domestic sales may rise, leaving us with an unambiguously positive change in welfare, but it is not certain that they will do so.

At this point, our conclusions are as follows:

1. Dumping is certain to lower welfare in the exporting nation whenever home sales fall and total output falls or remains constant, or whenever

   a. The firm trades under single pricing and the foreign market is perfectly competitive (Case Ib), or

   b. The firm trades under single pricing, has some monopoly power abroad, and total output remains constant or falls under dumping (Case IIIb).

2. Dumping is certain to raise welfare in the exporting nation whenever home sales rise or remain unchanged and total output rises, or whenever

   a. The firm does not trade under single pricing, will have some monopoly power abroad, and costs are falling or constant (Cases IIb and IIc).

3. Dumping may raise or lower welfare in the exporting nation whenever home sales fall and total output rises, or whenever

   a. The firm does not trade under single pricing and the foreign market is perfectly competitive (Case Ia),

   b. The firm does not trade under single pricing, will have some monopoly power abroad, and costs are rising (Case IIa), or

c. The firm trades under single pricing, has some monopoly power abroad, and output rises when dumping occurs (Case IIIa).

In all of these cases, however, our conclusions were reached under a set of assumptions that does not necessarily reflect reality. Thus, there exists the danger that dropping assumptions and returning to reality may destroy one or more of the definitive results derived above. There is, of course, also the possibility that the dissolution of limiting conditions may help clarify a case in which the welfare effect of dumping was indeterminate. Accordingly, we cannot stop at this point and offer our conclusions as a basis for evaluating current antidumping policy. Rather, in the next section I drop the assumptions underlying the previous analysis and describe how their absence affects the relationship between dumping and the changes in welfare established so far.

## Relaxing the Assumptions

Relaxing three of the assumptions underlying our model increases the probability that dumping will be beneficial under circumstances in which our results were inconclusive, but does no more than this. These are assumptions 5, that the firm's profit function has only one maximum; 6, that the feasible dumping margin is unlimited; and 1, that the economy is at full employment.

Assumptions 5 and 6 were introduced specifically to preclude complications raised in an article by W. W. Leontief. Leontief demonstrated that when dumping increases total output, home sales may rise even though marginal cost is increasing, if price discrimination is limited, or if it is unlimited and there is more than one local profit maximum.[15] In the previous discussion it was concluded that when dumping raised total output, welfare was certain to increase under some circumstances but could move in either direction under others. The reason for the indeterminate change in welfare in the latter circumstances was that dumping was certain to lower home sales, in some cases because marginal cost was rising. Thus, given Leontief's observations, dropping assumptions 5 and 6 makes dumping somewhat more likely to increase welfare than the previous analysis suggests. Moreover, although Leontief could not specify the probably frequency of the anomalous phenomenon that he discovered, it should be noted that in reality the dumping margin is usually limited by the height of tariff and transportation costs, and thus the conditions to which Leontief's findings pertain often exist.

The assumption that the economy operated at full employment was necessary to permit the firm's marginal cost to be used in evaluating the welfare changes wrought by dumping. For in a perfectly competitive, full-employment economy, marginal cost to any industry represents the dollar value of production sacrificed elsewhere to free resources for use in producing one last unit of its output. Marginal cost is, in other words, an accurate measure of the satisfaction foregone due to the production of one more unit of a dumped good.

In contrast, the state of the factor market in a situation of unemployment is illustrated in Figure 2–2. It is one in which factor prices are rigid downward at a real return per unit supplied of $(P_r/P^*)_1$, causing a present employment level of $N$ when suppliers desire to sell $S$. The real cost to society of the last unit of the factor employed is the supply price of the last unit hired, or $(P_r/P^*)_0$. As Figure 2–2 illustrates, the supply price for marginal units of the input lies below the present real market price over the entire range of unemployment $N - S$. Thus, when unemployment exists, the real cost to society of the employment of additional resources is less than their purchase price, unless the factor supply curve is perfectly elastic at the present market price. And, conversely, the real gain to society from the release of factors in any line of production is less than the money saving to the firm.

Thus, with respect to the present discussion, when unemployment exists, the dumper's private marginal cost curve necessarily lies above the true opportunity cost to society of incremental units of output. This does not alter our conclusion concerning the welfare effect of sales redistribution. This effect was calculated as the difference between foreign marginal revenue and the maximum home-demand price on each unit transferred and so did not involve marginal cost. However, the welfare effect of an increase in output due to dumping was assessed as the maximum home-demand price minus marginal cost for each new unit of domestic sales, and as foreign marginal revenue minus marginal cost for each added unit of exports. Conversely, the welfare effect of a fall in output was measured as $-(\bar{P}_h - MC)$ for each unit of domestic sales lost and as $-(MR_f - MC)$ for each unit decrease in foreign sales. Since private marginal cost exceeds social opportunity cost when unemployment exists, the rise in welfare consequent upon an expansion of output due to dumping and the fall in welfare from an output contraction will both be greater than when there is full employment.

Regarding the cases examined in the last section, we found that when dumping lowers output, welfare falls. Introducing unemployment into the model merely strengthens this conclusion. At the same time, however, we found in the instances in which the effect of dumping was beneficial or uncertain, that dumping increased total output. In all of these circumstances, the existence of unemployment will enlarge the benefits from output expansion; and thus unemployment weighs in favor of a rise in welfare in the indeterminate cases, although it cannot guarantee this result.

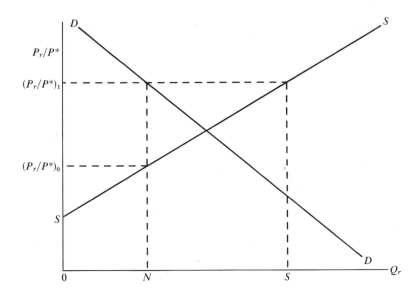

$P_r$ = the price of the resource.

$P^*$ = the average price of final-goods output.

**Figure 2–2.** Private Cost, Social Cost, and Unemployment in the Resource Market.

Relaxing assumption 3 (that resource prices paid by the dumper do not change as he expands or contracts production) has three ramifications for the conclusions of our model. When the dumper must increase factor prices in order to acquire resources, an expansion of output is accompanied by a rise in producer surplus; that is, in the rent acquired by intramarginal factors of production. This rent, which is included in the dumper's cost curves, represents a pure economic gain to productive factors in addition to the increase in profits that the dumper experiences. Since this second source of welfare gain to the exporting nation was precluded by assumption 3, when this assumption is dropped, dumping that increases output is more likely to increase welfare on balance than our model suggested, and dumping that lowers output is more likely to decrease welfare. Moreover, R. A. Cocks and H. G. Johnson have recently demonstrated that the sum of the increase in profits and producer surplus will always exceed the fall in consumer surplus that dumping generates when dumping creates trade and marginal cost rises because of rising factor prices.[16]

Consequently, since the Cocks-Johnson conditions apply to Cases Ia and IIIa, in which our results were inconclusive, the first and most important effect of dropping assumption 3 is to replace an ambiguous result with a certain increase in welfare in two circumstances. The second effect is to increase the probability that dumping will be beneficial to welfare in the remaining circumstance in which our model was inconclusive, since output rose therein. And the third effect is to reinforce the definitive results derived previously.

Dropping assumption 2 (that the economy is perfectly competitive except for the dumping industry) increases the probability that dumping will be detrimental to welfare in the indeterminate cases described above. For in all of the indeterminate cases, the dumper first redistributed sales away from the home market and then increased output and foreign sales. The effect of sales redistribution was always to lower welfare. The effect of output expansion was always to increase social welfare because additional output was produced and exported so long as foreign marginal revenue exceeded marginal cost, and the dumper's marginal cost equaled the true social cost of the additional exports. If the dumper bids resources away from industries that sell in monopolistic markets, however, his marginal cost will not represent the social opportunity cost of alternative output foregone. Rather, it will equal the marginal revenue sacrificed by the monopolies from which resources are drawn. Since the price of monopoly output exceeds marginal revenue, the true social sacrifice for an incremental unit of the dumper's goods will exceed his marginal cost.

In fact, it can be shown that the ratio of true social opportunity cost to the dumper's marginal cost will equal the weighted average degree of monopoly in the industries from which resources are acquired.

Let there be $i$ industries from which the dumper bids resources $R$, and let

$P_i$ = the price of final goods produced by $i$

$Q_i$ = the quantity of final goods produced by $i$

$P_r$ = the price of $R$

$R_i$ = the amount of $R$ used by $i$

$R_d$ = the amount of $R$ used by the dumper

$P_i/MC$ = the degree of monopoly pricing in $i$

$a_i$ = the percentage of $R$ used to produce one more unit of the dumpers output drawn from $i$

$\bar{P}/\overline{MC} = \Sigma_i a_i(P_i/MC_i)$ = the average degree of monopoly in the industries from which the dumper draws resources

$MC_d$ = the dumper's marginal cost

$\Delta W_i$ = the satisfaction lost from reduced consumption of industry $i$'s output for each one unit increase in the dumper's output

$\Delta W$ = the total social opportunity cost of one more unit of the dumper's output.

Then, for every small change in resource use needed to produce one more unit of the dumper's output, equations (2.19) follow:

$$\Delta W_i = P_i \frac{dQ_i}{dR_i} \frac{dR_i}{dR_d} dR_d$$

$$= \left(\frac{dR_i}{dR_d}\right) P_i \left(\frac{dQ_i / dR_i}{P_r}\right)(P_r \, dR_d)$$

$$\Delta W_i = a_i \frac{P_i}{MC_i} MC_d \tag{2.19}$$

$$\Delta W = \sum_i a_i \frac{P_i}{MC_i} MC_d = MC_d \sum_i a_i \frac{P_i}{MC_i}$$

$$\frac{\Delta W}{MC_d} = \frac{\bar{P}}{\overline{MC}}.$$

Thus, when the dumper acquires resources from monopolistic industries, the output-expansion step of the dumpiing process will yield a smaller increase in social welfare than otherwise; and, in fact, this step may compound the effect of sales redistribution by decreasing social welfare.

Moreover, in those cases in which an unambiguous increase in welfare from dumping was predicted, this prediction was based on the knowledge that within the confines of the model an increase in output always increased welfare. And, similarly, in those instances in which it was foreseen that dumping would lower welfare, this insight hinged on the fact that a fall in output always lowered welfare. When the true social cost of production exceeds the dumper's marginal cost, however, it is possible for it to exceed the home price or foreign marginal revenue, or both, existing after sales redistribution. Thus, a direct relationship between changes in output and welfare cannot be assumed. Consequently, a second and by far more significant effect of dropping assumption 2 is to destroy the definitive results previously reached.

When assumption 4 is relaxed and the dumper is permitted to produce intermediate inputs, our conclusions must be modified for two reasons. First, if the second-stage industry that purchases the dumper's output is itself a monopolistic seller, the demand curve faced by the dumper will be the user industry's marginal revenue product curve. The maximum demand price at which the dumper can sell any $i$th unit will then be the marginal revenue product of the $i$th unit in the fabricating industry. However, this understates the true social value of a marginal unit of the dumper's output, which would equal the maximum price at which additional "final" goods can be sold times the addition to final output yielded by the $i$th unit of resources. Thus, in using prices along the dumper's demand curve to discuss welfare, we will have underestimated any gain in welfare from a rise in home sales and any loss in welfare from a fall in home sales. Since we already know that dumping increases welfare whenever domestic sales rise, the former proposition holds little interest. However, in all cases in which the welfare effect of dumping was left in doubt, the doubt arose because home sales fell, reducing welfare, while output expanded, raising it. Thus, in these uncertain instances, when the dumper supplies an intermediate good, the possibility of a net welfare loss is amplified.

Second, in every instance discussed above (with the possible exception of Case IIc), the effect of dumping was to force domestic prices above the level of foreign levies. Thus as has often been stated, dumping by a primary-goods producer puts domestic user-industries at a cost disadvantage in facing rival foreign enterprises, both in competition in the domestic marketplace and in export markets. Resource dumping, then, must eventually be harmful to production and employment in advanced-stage industries even though such industries may be technologically efficient.

Finally, let us drop the assumption that dumping is done to maximize short-run profits and assume, instead, that it is done for long-run gains. If dumping to any extent raises present profits, we cannot say that the pricing policy is purely in the long-run interest of the firm. Thus, in considering the effect on welfare of dumping for long-run ends, we must start with the proposition that the producer has been given the option to dump and that at the outset he is either selling only at home, setting $MR_h = MC > MR_f$, or he is selling both at home and abroad, equating $MR_h = MR_f = MC$.

Our hypothesis then is that the firm is presently in a short-run, profit-maximizing position, with its home price above the foreign price, and that it wishes to increase foreign sales for predatory or other long-run reasons. The firm may increase foreign sales in two ways: by reducing domestic sales with output held constant or by raising output. Either alternative will permit the firm to initiate dumping or increase the present margin of discrimination.

The firm will acquire the additional goods it desires to dump in such a way that it minimizes the sacrifice of short-run profits. Thus, it will draw the next unit to be dumped from home sales whenever $MR_h$ is less than $MC$, and it will prefer to increase output whenever the reverse is true. Consequently, when engaging in predatory dumping, the producer behaves as he does in Case II above. If *MC* is rising, he will both increase total output and reduce home sales when dumping for long-run ends. If *MC* is constant, any additional dumping will come solely from augmented production. When *MC* is falling, the new dumped goods will come solely from an increase in output; and, in fact, nonprofit-maximizing dumping will make it worhthwhile for the dumper to expand home sales as well as exports.

Irrespective of the way in which the monopolist acquires the goods to export, by definition dumping for long-run gains diminishes short-run profits. Thus, in the eyes of the firm, the decision to dump predatorily, or to maintain market connections, or to gain entry into a foreign market is an investment decision. The cost of the investment is the present discounted value of the profits that must be foregone over a succession of years to accomplish its goals. The return is the present discounted value of the increase in profits from acquiring monopoly power abroad or attaining some other objective short of this. While the actual value of the cost and return stream may be considerably in doubt, the firm must feel that the expected rate of return exceeds the rate obtainable from alternative investments which could be made with the lost profits if it is to engage in the dumping policy under inspection. Thus, if the costs and benefits to society from such dumping were equal to the firm's costs and benefits, predatory and kindred dumping, unlike dumping to maximize short-run profits, would always benefit the exporting nation. As we have seen, however, the costs and benefits to the nation as a whole are not equal to those of the firm.

Regarding costs, the firm evaluates the amount invested in any year as the short-run profits sacrificed. If *MC* is constant, domestic consumption is unchanged by dumping to achieve long-run goals, and therefore the firm's cost and society's cost are one and the same. However, if *MC* is rising, home sales fall. There is a loss of consumer's surplus in addition to short-run profits, and social cost exceeds private cost. On the other hand, when *MC* is falling so that home sales rise with such dumping, the loss of monopoly profits is partially or wholly offset by a rise in consumer's surplus, and private cost exceeds social cost. Consequently, when *MC* rises, from society's point of view the monopolist will tend to overestimate the advisability of dumping predatorily or for lesser long-run goals, while he will underestimate the advisability of aggressive dumping when costs are decreasing.

Likewise, there is no reason for society's benefits to correspond to the long-run increase in the profits of the firm. However, since the potential difference between the two depends on changes in home and foreign sales that cannot be projected, it is difficult to say a priori whether the change in social welfare will exceed or fall short of the increase in monopoly profits.

## Conclusions

Like ivy, the preceding analysis has involved many intertwining branches of logic but has borne relatively little fruit. Nevertheless, it has yielded a few tender blossoms that bear on the rationality of present-day antidumping legislation. The analysis has shown that export dumping can increase or reduce welfare in the exporting nation. And it has shown that the effect of dumping depends on a wide variety of economic parameters that pertain to the firm's cost structure, the nature of home and foreign demand, and the state of the exporting nation's economy. In many instances, a specification of the general nature of these parameters left the welfare effect of dumping in doubt. In some instances, it yielded the conclusion that dumping definitely enhances or reduces welfare. It would be impossible, however, for administrators of legislation regulating export dumping to acquire the detailed data necessary to predict the welfare effect of dumping in those cases which have remained inconclusive. And the parameters which must be known to establish that dumping is certain to lower welfare are difficult, if not impossible, to discern. It is doubtful, for example, that one could tell in a given case of dumping whether the firm would have exported under single pricing or whether output is greater under dumping than otherwise. Consequently, while export dumping is a mixed gift to the exporting country, it is technically impossible to construct antidumping legislation to regulate the practice in a manner that maximizes welfare.

Although the absence of export-dumping regulations is a suboptimal policy, there is reason to believe that it is preferable to the total prevention that was recommended in the New Zealand resolution presented to the GATT. When dumping takes place in the present world economy, it is likely that the dumping margin will be limited by the level of tariffs and transport costs, that some unemployment will prevail at home, that the foreign market will be imperfectly competitive, or that the firm will face decreasing or constant costs and would not engage in trade if dumping were precluded. Each of these circumstances weights in favor of welfare-enhancing dumping; moreover, should the latter three obtain simultaneously, dumping will be certain to raise welfare. In fact, it is evident from Viner's description of American dumping at the turn of the century that these circumstances prevailed, and it was through witnessing dumping under these conditions that Fordney and other legislators may have concluded that dumping unambiguously benefits the exporting nation. In sum, in spite of this equivocal deduction on their part, the technical barriers to the optimal regulation of export dumping, combined with the likelihood that conditions amenable to beneficial dumping generally exist, makes the absence of export-dumping regulations in the United States Antidumping Act a reasonable commercial policy.

# Endnotes

1. U. S., Congress, House, 66th Cong., 2d sess., 9 December 1919, *Congressional Record* 59:329–30.

2. Gottfried von Haberler, *The Theory of International Trade* (London: William Hodge and Co., Ltd., 1935), chap. 6.

3. Jacob Viner, *Dumping: A Problem in International Trade* (Chicago: University of Chicago Press, 1923), p. 302.

4. Haberler, p. 302.

5. Y. O. Yntema, "The Influence of Dumping on Monopoly Price," *Journal of Political Economy* 36 (December 1928): 686–98.

6. Joan Robinson, *The Economics of Imperfect Competition* (London: Macmillan and Co., Ltd., 1933), bk. 5.

7. Two other publications are of only minor importance to the present subject but, nevertheless, should be mentioned in recapping the studies of dumping in relation to the exporting country. These are Kemp's short discussion of dumping as a tool of economic aggression and Simkin's discussion of price discrimination in general equilibrium; see Murray C. Kemp, *The Pure Theory of International Trade* (Englewood Cliffs, N. J.: Prentice-Hall, Inc., 1964), pp. 208–16; and C. G. F. Simkin, "Some Aspects and Generalizations of the Theory of Discrimination," *Review of Economic Studies* 15 (1974–48):1–13.

8. Steven Enke, "Monopolistic Output and International Trade," *Quarterly Journal of Economics* 60 (February 1946):233–37.

9. Ibid., pp. 236–37.

10. William Arthur Seavy, *Dumping since the War: The GATT and National Laws* (Oakland, Office Services Corp., 1970), pp. 5–6.

11. See H. W. de Jonge, "The Significance of Dumping in International Trade," *Journal of World Trade Law* 2 (1968):173–74; and Bart S. Fisher, "The Antidumping Law of the United States: A Legal and Economic Analysis," *Law and Policy in International Business* 5 (1973):89–90.

12. Fisher, p. 90.

13. Edwards derived this formula with a purely geometric model that made no reference to the conditions inherent in single pricing in two or more markets. The above proof incorporates his formula into the theory of price discrimination and shows how it arises from the logic of the practice. E. O. Edwards, "The Analysis of Output under Discrimination," *Econometrica* 18 (1950):163–72.

14. Robinson, p. 184.

15. W. W. Leontief, "The Theory of Limited and Unlimited Discrimination," *Quarterly Journal of Economics* 54 (May 1940):490–501.

16. R. A. Cocks and Harry G. Johnson, "A Note on Dumping and Social Welfare," *Canadian Journal of Economics* 1 (February 1972): 137–40.

# 3

## How the Importing Nation Should Regulate Dumping

Throughout the past century, there has persisted the general and amorphous feeling that dumping is an abnormal pricing strategy which bodes ill for the importing nation. As a result, dumping has been condemned on a variety of grounds, and many nations have legislated against it. In the present chapter, the case against dumping is evaluated from the importing society's point of view, and some general criteria for the proper regulation of the practice are derived. To a large extent, these criteria provide the framework within which the United States Antidumping Act is evaluated in later chapters.

In the first section, dumping is discussed in the context of the accepted body of international trade theory pertaining to normally priced imports. It is shown that dumping is not as extraordinary or malevolent a pricing policy as is commonly assumed, and some conclusions are reached concerning what a valid argument for antidumping legislation must demonstrate. In the next three sections, the claims against dumping that have been made in the past are inspected, and the chapter closes with some remarks on the form which optimal antidumping legislation should take.

### Dumping and the Theory of Trade Restrictions

Let us assume that we are looking at a static world economy in long-run equilibrium, that the nation under observation cannot affect the world market price of goods, and that the economy of this nation is perfectly competitive. It is axiomatic in the field of international trade that under these conditions national welfare will be greater under free trade than under either restricted or no trade. This conclusion may be demonstrated by considering the acts of importation and exportation simultaneously, using production possibility and indifference curves, or by inspecting either the market for importables or exportables, using demand and supply analysis. Figure 3–1 illustrates the argument from the point of view of importation.

Under autarchic production and consumption, a price of $P_a$ prevails in the national market, and a quantity $Q_a$ is purchased. Once trade is permitted, the domestic price of imports falls to the world market level and becomes $P_m$. Domestic producers react to this fall in price by cutting back

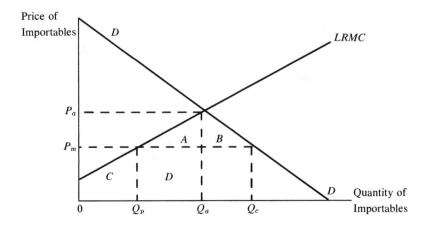

**Figure 3–1.** Demand and Supply in an Import Market.

production until marginal cost equals $P_m$, or to $Q_p$. Since $P_m$ represents the resource cost of obtaining importables through exportation, in effect domestic producers forego the manufacture of all units of importables for which the resource cost of direct production exceeds the cost of obtaining the goods through trade. Consequently, whereas before trade the total value of resources employed in obtaining $Q_a$ importables was equal to areas $A + C + D$, after trade it is equal to areas $C + D$ alone. In total, the economy maintains its old level of importables consumption while saving resources equivalent to area $A$ to be employed in expanding output for domestic use.

Consumers in turn expand their purchase of importables to $Q_c$. The dollar value of satisfaction gained for each additional unit of importable consumed is equal to the maximum price at which that unit will just be purchased, as indicated by the demand curve. The value of satisfaction foregone due to the reduction in the consumption of other goods per unit of importable purchased is represented by the price of the importable. Consequently, consumers increase their purchase of importables as long as the welfare gain from importables consumption exceeds the welfare loss from the reduced consumption of other goods necessary to enlarge exportation. In total, the net increase in welfare due to the change in the consumer market basket is equal to area $B$.

Through its effect on the pattern of production and consumption, trade raises national welfare above the level obtaining in isolation by a value equal to areas $A + B$. As one part of the process of trade, importation increases welfare, and, as is apparent from the graph, the lower the price of its importables, the more the nation benefits. Moreover, given our initial assumptions, any restriction on imports will reduce welfare because it will cause domestic production to be substituted for imports when importation is the cheaper method of acquisition, and it will force consumers to reduce the purchase of importables and forego, in part, the addition to consumer surplus that importation generated. At least, these conclusions are valid when the imports are normally priced; that is, sold at identical prices in the markets of all nations.

Suppose, however, that rather than being sold at identical prices in all markets, the importables were dumped. Would this suggest that in making foreign sales, the exporting concerns were differently motivated than firms which did not price discriminate in trade? Would it thereby indicate that something extraordinary and perhaps a bit sinister was taking place in the import market: something that could not be integrated into the above model without disturbing its bucolic appearance? Apparently not, for J. Robinson has shown that a profit-maximizing monopolist who is capable of separating markets will charge identical prices at home and abroad only if the demand curves in the two markets have equal elasticities.[1] Even then, marginal distribution, marketing, and other nonproduction costs relating to sales in the individual markets must be the same for equal prices to arise.[2] Thus, when a firm's goal is profit maximization, the appearance of identical prices in separate markets will be a freak of nature. One would expect dumping to occur regularly as a somewhat innocuous practice, with the forces leading to price discrimination being no different than those that induce any monopolist to choose one price level over another.

Would the introduction of dumping change the effect of importation on welfare in the importing nation? From a qualitative point of view, again the answer is no. The only assumptions necessary to establish the proposition that free trade maximizes welfare are that the importing economy is perfectly competitive, that it must take the terms of trade as data, and that the imports provide a continuing source of supply. Economic conditions outside of the importing nation, including the relationship between the import price and the home price in the exporting country, are irrelevant. For regardless of whether the home price is greater than, less than, or equal to the export price, the price in the importing nation will still be permanently lower when importation occurs, and the subsequent change in consumption, production, and welfare will be the same.

From a quantitative point of view, however, the analysis of the previous chapter suggests that the answer is yes, since the analysis showed that import prices will generally be lower under dumping than single pricing and that the volume of imports will be greater. Hence, we may conclude that the lesson of the traditional, competitive-equilibrium model—that free trade is generally preferable to restricted trade—applies to dumped as well as to nondumped goods. And we may further note, within the context of this model, that permitting dumping is preferable to a policy of enforced single pricing.

Of course, a perfectly competitive, static-equilibrium model is unrealistic. It does not tell the whole story of the effect of normal imports on welfare, nor is it intended to do so. One cannot draw the conclusion from the model that the importing which will occur under realistic conditions will always benefit the importing nation. One cannot conclude, posthaste, that importing should be unregulated. Nevertheless, the impact of the model on economic thinking has been to establish an a priori case for free trade and to place the burden of proof on those who would regulate importation. And in the same sense, since the idealized model shows unrestricted dumping to raise welfare in the importing nation, it establishes a presumption in favor of permitting dumping. It shifts the burden of proof to those who support restraints on dumping and makes it incumbent upon them to demonstrate that dumping injures the importing society.

To establish a case for antidumping legislation, however, it is not enough to demonstrate that dumping harms welfare in the importing nation under a given set of conditions. By dropping the assumptions of the idealized model, economists have shown that permitting free importation in general may be a suboptimal commercial policy in a number of circumstances. Overall, they have tendered four major reasons that unregulated importation can be detrimental to the importing country. First, although free trade raises a nation's welfare above the level obtained in isolation, further gains may be had if limiting imports changes the terms of trade. This line of reasoning is the basis for the optimum tariff argument and for the broad exhortation to governments to induce their citizens to act as monopsonists in purchasing foreign goods.[3] Second, dynamic considerations, omitted from the static model, may make importation injurious in itself. Unstable imports may do more harm by disrupting markets than good by encouraging specialization and expanding consumers options. Or, as in the infant industry argument, the pattern of importation established under free trade may prevent the national (and world) economy from developing in the most efficient manner.[4] Third, normative goals may outweigh considerations of economic efficiency as a basis for commercial policy. Particular import transactions may be inequitable. They may have inequitable side effects. Or, as the Stolper-Samuelson principle suggests, importation may result in an undesirable redistribution of income.[5] Fourth, in all probability the importing economy will not be perfectly competitive. In this and the preceding two instances, restricted trade may be preferable to free trade if corrective policy options are limited.

Moreover, as was the case in the preceding static-equilibrium analysis, the arguments for import restrictions make no reference to the relationship between the import price and the price in the producing country, for their validity is not affected by the presence of price discrimination between national markets. The optimum tariff argument, for example, depends only on the assumption of an imperfectly elastic foreign offer curve. The argument for import restrictions due to market disruptions hinges only on the temporary nature of the imports. Even the arguments based on the existence of monopoly refer only to monopoly in the importing country.

Mainstream writings in international trade have demonstrated that the unencumbered importation of both dumped and nondumped goods is undesirable in a number of circumstances. Yet, to the extent that dumped and nondumped imports do not differ in their ramifications for economic welfare, there is no need for statutes directed specifically at dumping. Consequently, advocates of antidumping acts cannot prove their case simply by maintaining that dumping harms the importing nation. Rather, they must also show that the welfare consequences of dumping are significantly different from those of normal imports. Thus, a valid argument for antidumping legislation must demonstrate the validity of at least one of three propositions: (1) that dumping lowers welfare in some circumstances in which normal imports do not; (2) that dumped imports have exactly the same detrimental effect on welfare as single-priced imports, but, because of the nature of dumped goods, they escape existing sanctions; (3) that both dumped and normal imports may injure welfare in a given situation; however, the injury is more likely to occur, or will be quantitatively greater, in the case of dumped goods; and it can be expected that the harm done by dumped imports will be significant, while the harm done by normal imports will be less than the administrative cost of prevention.

Noticeably, under the first two propositions it is maintained that dumping is a unique phenomenon which is either peculiarly injurious or particularly difficult to regulate. The third proposition, however, does not make this claim. Rather, it justifies special legislation regulating dumping on the basis of expected benefits and costs, and thus provides the weakest and most speculative argument for an antidumping act, however, valid. Nevertheless, as shown in the pages below, to a great extent the supportable case for antidumping legislation is based on this tenet.

## An Evaluation of the Case for
## Antidumping Legislation

The arguments against dumping may be classified in a number of ways. For example, some opponents of dumping object to price discrimination in itself. Some find dumping odious because it is likely to involve less-than-cost pricing, while others contend that dumping is harmful because of the increased flexibility in setting export prices that it gives producers. Thus, one basis for classifying complaints against dumping is the characteristic of the practice that is the source of the complaint. As mentioned above, a second basis for classifying arguments against dumping is the distinction drawn between dumped and ordinary imports in support of legislation that governs dumped imports alone. These facets of the arguments against dumping are of some interest, and each is noted in the discussion below. Still, the purpose of the present chapter is to ascertain how dumping should be regulated; and thus in the following pages, the arguments against dumping are grouped according to the type of prohibitions thay they recommend. In all, eight complaints against dumping have been made with some frequency in the past. Six of these espouse an absolute prohibition of the practice. One advocates measures against dumping whenever it injures domestic producers, and one advocates such measures when dumping has an anticompetitive effect on the import market.

### The Case for Prohibiting All Dumping

Of the arguments that have been used to espouse the prohibition of all dumping, four assert that price discrimination in itself is harmful to the importing nation. In two of these arguments, the speaker does not bother to differentiate the effects of dumped and normal imports. Rather, he merely identifies an injury to the importing nation that occurs when dumping takes place. Due to the speaker's lack of circumspection, however, the injury attributed to dumping is identical to that which occurs under ordinary importation. Moreover, when normal imports cause the injury, it is commonly held in the literature on commercial policy that barriers to trade are not an appropriate remedy. Thus, in reality not only are measures against dumping alone unwarranted, but they are a particularly ill-advised solution to the problem at hand.

For example, lately opponents of dumping, on rare occasions, have mentioned that dumping hurts the importing nation's balance of payments. Typically, this claim has been mentioned as an aside during the discussion of other, more significant injuries such as a decrease in profits, sales, or employment in the import-competing industry.Apparently, it represents little more than an attempt by the speaker to muster all of the counts against dumping imaginable.[6]

In what sense, we may ask, does dumping harm the importer's balance of payments any more than the importation of articles identically priced in all markets? The substitution of dumping for single pricing will usually increase the money value of imports because the dumper always sells along the elastic portion of his foreign demand curve. For exactly the same reason, however, the balance of payments will move toward deficit should a single price monopolist reduce his export price. On the other hand, if exporters are perfect competitors in all markets, they may trade at a price on the inelastic section of a nation's import demand curve; and in this situation a price decline will reduce the outpayments made by an importing country. But as long as the import-demand curve is elastic within the range of the price change, the transition from single pricing to dumping affects the importing nation's balance of payments no differently than, say, an equal fall in prices due to technological advances abroad. Thus, in the absence of other arguments, there is no more reason to sanction dumping to improve the balance of payments than there is to sanction normal imports.

Consequently, antidumping duties are an exceedingly inappropriate remedy for a balance-of-payments deficit. Given the similartiy between dumped and ordinary imports, an antidumping duty levied for the purpose of erasing a payments deficit would amount to no more than a selective tariff. Yet, in terms of welfare maximization, it is generally acknowledged that tariffs are inferior to devaluation and other methods of balancing payments because they distort consumer choices, thereby creating an excess burden in addition to the necessary welfare loss from disabsorption. On this score, then, antidumping duties and a general tariff on all imports would be equally ill conceived.

In addition, all tariffs invite retaliation from nations whose exports are impaired, and retaliation is more likely to ensue when the tariff is selective and discriminatory. Because they constitute a selective tariff when used to balance payments—and, in fact, are a rather devious approach to the problem—antidumping duties are more likely to be met with retaliatory measures than is a general import duty. Moreover, if the retaliation is in kind, as it is likely to be, it will be particularly harmful to deficit nations whose relatively high internal prices have led to both a payments deficit and extensive dumping on the part of their exporters. Aside from the fact that antidumping duties, like tariffs, are an inferior means of balancing payments, antidumping duties are more likely to have disadvantageous ramifications for a nation's exports and are thereby less likely to succeed in accomplishing their objective.

Akin to the balance-of-payments argument is the contention that antidumping duties should be used as a palliative for unemployment. In his lengthy article on dumping, B. S. Fisher observes that temporary dumping is generally condemned by economic theorists while persistent dumping is customarily deemed beneficial to the importing nation because it provides a dependable supply of cheap imports. However, Fisher asserts that there are, in fact, reasons for condemning even continuous dumping. According to Fisher, one count against persistent dumping is that we do not have a frictionless economy that guarantees full employment; and when dumping lowers employment, the benefits to the importing nation are less than is usually assumed.[7] While this may be true, it must be observed that what has been said about the relationship between dumping and the balance of payments pertains equally to the effect of dumping on employment. The effect of persistent dumping on employment is no different from that produced by stable importation under single pricing, and there is no more reason to selectively regulate continuous dumping to remedy unemployment than there is to reduce the volume of ordinary imports. Moreover, it is the responsibility of governments to maintain employment with fiscal, monetary, and kindred measures, and not with restrictive trade policies that, for the reasons discussed above, are decidedly inferior methods of achieving this goal.

The third argument in which price discrimination is described as injurious to the importing nation involves the semiarchaic claim that dumping and undervaluation are equivalent acts. This misconception surfaced in 1913 when the change from specific to ad valorem duties aroused concern about the fraudulent misrepresentation of import prices. Those who recommended that an antidumping statute be included in American import regulations maintained that dumping, like undervaluation, was a misrepresentation of the dutiable value of imports, and that it was done to avoid tariffs, thereby resulting in a subversion of the tariff structure.[8]

Of course there is no truth to the first proposition. Dumping is a simply the sale of goods for export at a price below prices in the home country. Neither the home price nor the export price is necessarily falsified on the sales invoice under dumping any more than such prices are necessarily falsified on invoices pertaining to normal imports. If the basis for duty collection is the home-market value of the imports, dumping may lead to an erroneous assessment, but only through an equivocation on the part of the customs appraiser who mistakenly takes the sales price as representative of the home-market price.

With respect to the second proposition, tariffs lower the net price that an exporter can charge while maintaining a given volume of sales. Because of this, exporters generally react to higher tariffs by lowering both their price and sales volume. Exporters react in this manner, not to avoid the tariff, but because lower net demand dictates a change in policy in order to achieve the customary goals of the firm, be they profit maximization, market-share maintenance, or what have you. This is true both of exporters who are dumpers and those who are not, the only difference being that the dumper may lower his price in the export market without reducing it elsewhere. Consequently, it cannot be maintained that dumpers are more likely to lower prices in response to a tariff than are other exporters, nor can it be said that dumped goods escape the taxation intended under a general tariff any more than do ordinary imports.

Finally, consider the following remarks of Mr. Byrnes, made before Congress in 1965.

The antidumping law is supposed to protect domestic industry from the unfair practice of a foreign competitor offering a commodity for sale in this country at a price lower than he offers it in the markets of the world or his home market. This results in unfair competition with domestic industry. At times foreign items are even offered for sale below their cost of production.[9]

In Mr. Byrnes's view, the sole benchmark of commercial fairness is the producer's home price, and any levy less than this price is unfairly low. Consequently, dumping can be differentiated from normal importation and condemned simply because it is the act of price discrimination, which is inherently unethical. Yet, this description of dumping certainly rests on a curious interpretation of fairness, for the home price of the dumper is necessarily a monopoly price. From the seller's side of the market, it is difficult to understand why the offering of goods in exportation at a price below the restrictive home price necessarily results in unfair competition from import-competing industries.

On the other hand, from the consumer's point of view, economists generally hold that a monopoly price is unfair because it exceeds the price that would exist under an efficient resource allocation determined by impersonal market forces, and it results in a forced redistribution of income from consumers to producers. Consequently, the dumper's home price is an exploitative price, and, ironically, to require its enforcement in the import market would enlarge the domain of monopolistic exploitation. It is no wonder, then, that while Mr. Byrnes calls dumping unethical, he fails to explain the basis for his normative judgment; for attention to this aspect of the problem reveals that dumping prevents, rather than produces, unfair import pricing.

In the two remaining arguments for prohibiting all dumping, price discrimination is not decried as inherently injurious or unethical in itself. Rather, dumping is opposed because it usually results in the pricing of exports below the cost of production. In these arguments, this property of dumping distinguishes it from ordinary exportation. According to the first, less-than-cost pricing makes dumping harmful to the importing nation's welfare and to world welfare, while normal importation is not. According to the second, it makes dumping an unethical marketing practice.

In a recent journal article, R. A. Anthony provided an exhaustive explanation of why dumping should be condemned as detrimental to welfare on the basis of the cost-price relationship that the practice entails.[10] According to Anthony, the law of comparative advantage states that prices will be minimized throughout the world when international trade occurs along the lines of relative productive efficiency. Thus, whenever a manufacturer can sell in foreign markets more cheaply than native producers because he "possesses material or earned advantages," he should be permitted to do so. But an exporter should not be permitted to undersell domestic producers when his low price arises from an artificial advantage rather than cost-efficient production.[11]

The dumper in turn possesses monopoly power in his home market that permits him to charge a higher price than would arise under competitive conditions, and it is because of this monopoly power that the dumper can export at low prices. Of course, the dumper's low export price may exceed his average total cost, and, if this is the case, any underselling in foreign markets will be due to the dumper's comparative advantage in production. But the dumper's export price may also be less than average total cost, since his high domestic price permits him to recoup more than a proportional share of fixed costs on home sales. When such export pricing occurs, domestic buyers, in effect, subsidize the dumper's exportation. The low export price does not arise from the legitimate advantage of low-cost production. Rather, it is attributable to the dumper's domestic monopoly position.[12]

Moreover, the dumper's home monopoly position, and not cost efficiency, will be the causative factor behind his low export price often enough to condemn dumping as generally contrary to comparative advantage. The dumper may charge an export price that is less than the average marginal cost of producing in excess of home demand.[a] When such a price obtains, it does not matter whether costs are rising or falling, or whether we are considering a short-run or long-run production decision. The revenue garnered from export sales will not be sufficient to cover the direct costs attributable to exportation, no less their fair share of fixed costs. Thus, selling at such a price will require the subsidization of exports either from abnormal profits earned at home or through the incursion of a net loss by the dumper, and trade will assuredly run counter to comparative advantage.[13]

On the other hand, the dumper's foreign price may exceed the average marginal cost of producing exports. In this case, it cannot be said that the exports are subsidized in the short run, for the only relevant costs in deciding the short-run level of prices and sales are variable costs; and, hence, in the short run, exportation at a price in excess of per-unit variable cost is profitable in itself. However, neither can it be said that the dumper possesses a comparative advantage on such sales, for the short-run period is too brief to decide if such an advantage exists. Rather, in deciding the merit of the dumper's export price, we must examine that

[a] This cumbersome terminology is necessary because Anthony confuses the concepts of marginal and average variable cost. As a result, he speaks of the marginal cost of exports when he means the average variable cost attaching specifically to export production, where exports are always the last units of output produced. See Anthony as cited in Fndnote 10, pp. 170–80 passim.

price from the point of view of the long-run production decision, encompassing as it does the issue of contracting for fixed costs.[14]

In the long run, when production occurs under conditions of rising cost, if the dumper's export price exceeds the average marginal cost of producing additional output for export sale, it will probably also exceed average total cost. For when marginal cost is rising, the range of output over which it is less than average total cost is decidedly brief. Thus, when costs are rising, the foreign price will probably be a full-cost price, and underselling by the dumper in foreign markets will probably be based on his comparative cost efficiency. However, we may discount this case as relatively unimportant, for when costs are rising, exportation quickly equates marginal cost and foreign marginal revenue. Consequently, only decreasing cost producers will continuously dump appreciable quantities abroad.[15]

When costs fall with output, average total cost will be continually above the average marginal cost of producing for export. Thus, even if the dumper's export price remains above the average variable cost of exports, there is the ever present danger that it will fall short of average total cost. Moreover, not only does this possibility exist, but there are two reasons for believing that the export price will be below average total cost except in rare instances.[16]

First, when the dumper is a profit maximizer—as he is likely to be in the long run—declining cost, in and of itself, encourages the pricing of exports below unit cost. For in the case of rising cost, dumping is profitable only because a net profit is earned on each unit of exports. But when costs are falling, the expansion of output that furnishes goods for dumping abroad also reduces the average total cost of domestic sales. Thus, dumping is secondarily and indirectly profitable because it "makes home sales more remunerative." Consequently, the dumper will find it advantageous to reduce export prices below average total cost, thereby raising the quantity exported, as long as the additional profit from home sales created by declining average total cost counterbalances the additional loss on export sales.[17]

Second, falling costs often encourage an overexpansion of capacity relative to home demand. Subsequently, competition for sales reduces the home price below average total cost, creating a chronically "sick" industry in which firms cannot recapture fixed costs and are left to minimize their losses. While trying to survive the period in which price competition reduces capacity, producers sell at home as long as the domestic price covers the average variable cost of producing for the home market, and they dump abroad as long as the foreign price exceeds the average variable cost of producing for export. Under these conditions, of course, export sales at a price below cost will not be made indefinitely. Such sales, however, may be forthcoming for an extended period of time. And these export sales will not only fail to recapture their full unit cost, they will not contribute to the recovery of fixed costs at the same rate as domestic purchases.[18] Thus, both the producer and consumers in the country of manufacture will be subsidizing the exports.

In summary, dumping can engender a low export price that does not involve a subsidy based on monopoly control of the domestic market. The dumper may sell abroad at a price above average total cost in the short run. He may export at such a price in the long run when producing along the rising portion of his marginal cost curve. He may even establish a full-cost export price in the long run when faced with increasing returns.

However, overall, the importing nation will not benefit substantially from instances in which the dumping price covers unit cost. For when the unsubsidized export price is a short-run phenomenon, the importing nation does not acquire a dependable supply of cheap goods. When such a price is established in the long run under conditions of increasing cost, an appreciable quantity of goods will not be exported. And although it would involve the sale of a significant quantity of import, the emergence of a full-cost price under decreasing cost conditions is extremely unlikely.

Rather, in most instances in which costs are declining and dumping continuously fosters a substantial supply of importables, the price of imports will be less than the average total cost production. In these instances, the imports will not recoup their pro-rata share of fixed costs but will be subsidized through the redemption of a greater than pro-rata share of fixed costs at home. Producers of import-competing goods, who must recover all costs in their home market, will be undersold; not because the exporter is a more efficient producer, but because he possesses an illegitimate advantage owing to his domestic monopoly position. To the extent that the exporter acquires foreign sales by dumping, production will not occur according to the dictates of comparative advantage. And thus on this basis, a general prohibition of dumping, including continuous dumping, may rightfully be enacted.[19]

As stated by Anthony, the "comparative advantage' argument against dumping contains three propositions: (1) that dumping differs from single pricing because it allows producers to price exported goods below cost, either continuously or for an extended period of time; (2) that the long-run price under dumping will usually be lower than the average cost of production; and (3) that, because of this, dumping will disrupt the flow of trade according to comparative advantage, thereby injuring welfare in the importing nation and the world at large. We can assess the validity of the comparative-advantage argument for prohibiting dumping by evaluating the merit of each of these propositions.

With respect to the first proposition, when the monopolist can earn a normal profit by producing for the home market, one can safely say that a single pricer will never choose to export at a price below cost; for, in this instance, pricing below unit cost in the export market would require the incursion of an absolute loss. Such a policy could not be maintained in the long run, nor would it be a logical choice as an alternative to positive profits. It is imaginable, in the extreme, that a single pricer could adopt such a policy in the short run if, by charging a low export price, he could gain entry into a new market, improve his foreign market share, or even monopolize the foreign market. But it is highly improbable that a firm could bankroll the losses required to achieve substantial market entry or that it would be willing to move from black to red on its present income statement to obtain uncertain gains in its export position.

On the other hand, the option to dump severs the link between the domestic and foreign markets forged by the necessity of maintaining equal prices. Consequently, when home-market sales are profitable, the firm will be able to establish a price below unit cost in either the short or long run without endangering its existence, and it may choose to do so either because profit maximization dictates such a policy or because an export price of this nature is needed to achieve other ends. Thus, dumping gives the firm an option that it does not possess when forced to maintain price equality. From this standpoint, the ability to dump definitely alters the kinds of pricing behavior to be expected from the firm.

If domestic sales are unprofitable, however, the theoretics of Chapter 2 indicate that a single-price monopolist as well as a dumper may export at a price below cost, for it was shown that a single-price monopolist can find exportation to be profit maximizing (or loss minimizing) even if foreign prices are below the optimal domestic price. To reiterate the discussion therein, let us assume that home demand has fallen to $D_h$ in Figure 3–2.

Given this demand curve, the loss-minimizing domestic price in autarky is $P_0$. If the single pricer wishes to export, he must lower his home price to $P_1$. In order to do so, however, he must expand domestic sales to $Q_1$, thereby incurring an additional loss on domestic sales equal to area $A$. At the same time, by lowering the domestic price to $P_1$ he will acquire the opportunity to export as long as foreign marginal revenue exceeds marginal cost, and he may thus export an amount $Q_2 - Q_1$. On these goods he will earn a net profit that reduces his losses by area $B$. If we assume that areas $A$ and $B$ are equal, the single-price monopolist will just be indifferent to exporting at a price less than average total cost when demand has fallen to the level $D_h$. If demand has fallen farther than this, area $B$ would be larger and area $A$ smaller, and thus the single-price monopolist would engage in exportation. Consequently, when home demand is depressed, a firm may export at a price less than unit cost even if it cannot dump, and

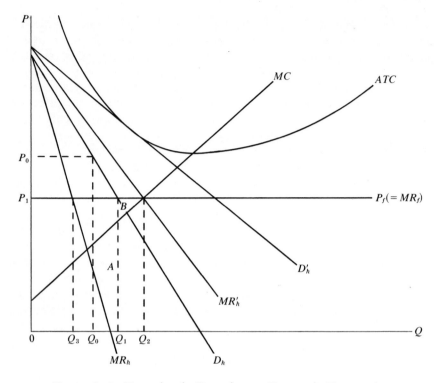

**Figure 3–2.** Dumping in Reaction to Domestic Depression.

dumping cannot be said to be necessary for less-than-cost pricing in exportation by chronically depressed industries.

Nevertheless, it was shown in Chapter 2 that a firm which can dump will commence exporting as soon as the maximum foreign price equals home marginal revenue at the profit-maximizing level of domestic output. Consequently, in the above graph, a dumper would have started to export at a price below cost when demand fell to $D'_h$. Moreover, when demand had reached the level $D_h$, he would have exported quantity $Q_2 - Q_3$. Thus, as a result of domestic depression, less-than-cost pricing in export trade will be much more likely and will involve larger quantities when dumping is permitted than when it is not. With one qualification, then, Anthony was correct in asserting that export pricing below cost is the domain of the dumper alone.

As to the second plank in the comparative-advantage argument, it is tautological that a dumper will price below cost in export trade whenever he prices below average cost at home. Thus, the only pertinent question is, will a dumper also regularly price below unit cost abroad when a profit can be earned in the domestic market? With respect to this issue, Anthony admits that the dumper's long-run export price will generally exceed average total cost when he is producing under rising cost conditions. Consequently, the proposition that a dumper will usually price below cost hinges on Anthony's assertion that such a price can be expected to obtain when costs are decreasing and that only under decreasing-cost conditions will a substantial and dependable supply of exports be made available.

Anthony's explanation of why a dumper will normally price below cost in foreign markets under decreasing-cost conditions, however, is equivocal. Anthony states that a dumper is likely to carry foreign sales to a point where they are unprofitable because the accompanying expansion of output and fall in per-unit cost raises the amount of profits earned at home. Yet, it was shown in Chapter 2 that a dumper maximizes profits by producing and distributing output between two markets so that $MC = MR_h = MR_f$. Regardless of whether average total cost is rising or falling, this condition determines the optimal quantity of home and foreign sales and the corresponding prices to be charged in each market. Thus, the profit-maximizing export price is determined solely by the shape of the domestic and foreign demand curves and the dumper's marginal cost curve. It is not influenced by the dumper's average total cost curve. And the fact that the average total cost of home sales may decrease as output grows will not give the dumper an incentive to enlarge the quantity that he exports.

Moreover, by utilizing the knowledge that a profit-maximizing dumper equates foreign marginal revenue to marginal cost in equilibrium, we can describe the condition under which the dumper's export price will fall short of average total cost. This condition indicates that a dumper is no more likely to price exports below cost than he is to price them above unit cost, when costs are falling. Letting $\eta_f$ equal the elasticity of the foreign demand curve and $\eta_a$ the elasticity of the dumper's average total cost curve, equations (3.1) are obtained:

$$MR_f = P_f\left(1 + \frac{1}{\eta_f}\right),$$

$$MC = d\{(ATC)Q_t\}/dQ_t = (ATC) + Q_t\frac{d(ATC)}{dQt}$$

$$= (ATC)\left(1 + \frac{1}{\eta_a}\right). \tag{3.1}$$

Thus, when the dumper equates $MC$ and $MR_f$, equations (3.2) follow:

$$P_f\left(1 + \frac{1}{\eta_f}\right) = (ATC)\left(1 + \frac{1}{N_a}\right), \quad \text{or}$$

$$\frac{P_f}{(ATC)} = \frac{\eta_f\eta_a + \eta_f}{\eta_f\eta_a + \eta_a}. \tag{3.2}$$

Consequently, $P_f \gtreqless ATC$ according as $|\eta_a| \gtreqless |\eta_f|$. The foreign price established by the dumper producing under decreasing-cost conditions will be greater or less than his per-unit cost according as the elasticity of his long-run average total cost curve at the equilibrium level of total output is greater or less than the elasticity of foreign demand at the equilibrium level of export sales. In order to claim that a decreasing-cost producer will usually export at a price below cost, we must have some basis for expecting a priori that $|\eta_a| < |\eta_f|$ in long-run equilibrium.

Can it be anticipated that in the usual instance $|\eta_f|$ will exceed $|\eta_a|$ in equilibrium? The fact that a dumper exports a volume of goods at which the foreign demand curve is elastic supports this notion and lends credence to Anthony's assertion. So too does the observation that the dumper will customarily face an elastic demand curve in the foreign market because of the existence of import-competing producers, But at the same time, econometric studies suggest that the long-run average total cost curves of mass-production enterprises are normally highly elastic over a wide range of output and take on low elasticity values only when output is small.[20] Thus, one would expect that dumpers will regularly charge a foreign price that does not cover unit cost in a number of circumstances. They will tend to do so when production in an industry subject to scale economies remains dispersed among a large number of firms. They will tend to do so if domestic demand is not great enough to permit the attainment of scale economies by domestic concerns, and producers primarily build capacity with an eye to the domestic market. Both of these conditions are not likely to obtain, however, and in their absence it cannot be maintained that dumpers in decreasing-cost industries will generally establish a long-run export price deficient to recoup the average total cost of exports.

Finally, it cannot be said that a dumper who charges an export price less than his per-unit cost, and who acquires foreign sales by undercutting import-competing producers, necessarily sells in contradiction to the law of comparative advantage, nor that he thereby lowers welfare in the importing country. First, even if the dumper's foreign-market price is less than his long-run average total cost, and , in addition, the price charged by his foreign rivals, the dumper's per-unit cost may still be less than the minimum average total cost attainable abroad. Exportation at a price less than long-run unit cost does not preclude the possibility that the dumper, in fact, possesses a comparative cost advantage, nor does it weigh against this possibility. It merely reflects the fact that export sales cannot be made at the dumper's domestic monopoly price.

Second, an export price that is less than the average total cost of the dumper may have other characteristics that operate to the detriment of the importing nation. But the importation of dumped goods at such a price cannot be condemned because it results in the substitution of a high-cost source of supply for low-cost domestic output. To the importing nation, the resource cost of an import is equal to its supply price, not the per-unit cost of foreign production. Other considerations aside, the importing country does not care whether a low import price is predicated on comparative cost efficiency or upon a governmental export bounty or other subsidy. In either case, through importation, the nation will benefit from the low price through the consumer and producer effects described at the beginning of this chapter.

Thus, if the export price is less than the lowest level of average total cost attainable by domestic producers, the importing nation will unambiguously benefit from importation through an expansion of consumer surplus and the saving of resources, even though the exporter does not possess a comparative advantage. If the import price is less than the current level of per-unit cost of domestic producers, but not less than the lowest level attainable, the imports may prevent an expansion in domestic production that would benefit the importing country. In this instance, the importing nation could be said to be injured by importation contrary to comparative advantage, but this statement would be equally valid if the import price was a full-cost price. The correct remedy, then, is not the institution of antidumping duties but, as suggested by the infant industry argument, a temporary tariff that permits the expansion of domestic industry until it becomes price competitive.

Moreover, in terms of the dictates of comparative advantage theory for world welfare, the world is not necessarily worse off when dumping fosters the flow of goods in trade in opposition to relative cost efficiency. The principle that the movement of trade in accordance with comparative advantage maximizes world welfare pertains only to a situation in which all markets are perfectly competitive, while dumping requires monopoly in the home market. Thus, the tenets of comparative advantage cannot automatically be assumed to operate in a world in which dumping takes place, and, in fact, they are not generally applicable. Rather, as has been demonstrated in Chapter 2, the exporting nation as well as the importing nation may benefit from the replacement of a regime of single pricing with dumping, regardless of whether the export price is greater or less than average total cost. Among other things, the onset of dumping may lower the price charged at home and simultaneously enlarge the exportation of goods on which foreign marginal revenue exceeds the marginal social cost of production. Consequently, one cannot maintain that dumping contrary to cost efficienty will necessarily raise the average price of supply on a universal basis, or that it will necessarily lower world welfare, or that the importing nation will benefit at the expense of the exporting nation.

Nevertheless, as a corollary to the above arguments, some opponents of dumping have claimed that the practice is unethical because it normally entails less-than-cost pricing.[21] They have asserted that in the realm of business, persons are sometimes so related that ethical conduct requires that they be treated equally. Buyers, for example, should not be forced to pay different prices. And competing sellers should not be given an "artificial" advantage over their rivals regardless of the consequent benefit to the well-being of society. Dumping in turn confers such an advantage on exporting concerns, because it permits them to price below cost by expensing an inordinate amount of fixed costs on home sales while import-competing producers must recover all costs in their domestic market. Consequently, since less-than-cost pricing is characteristic of dumping, the practice should be prohibited on moral grounds.

Of course, a number of moral tenets of this argument are open to question. First, it is not entirely obvious on moral grounds why domestic concerns should be protected from an "artificial," or man-made, advantage given to foreign producers and not an advantage derived from nature. For example, why should domestic concerns be shielded from the effects of a foreign export subsidy and not from that of low foreign wages. The economist's answer is that foreign export bounties raise the threat of monopolization and, at the same time, may cause wasteful production shifts because they are temporary. In contrast, low foreign wages do not augur monopoly and are usually the cause of a permanent supply of cheap imports. But this answer involves considerations of economic efficiency and not morality. Such considerations aside, however, economists have adhered to the notion that there is no more reason to sanction bountied imports than imports whose cheapness is derived from low foreign wages. On the other hand, in the past businessmen have often claimed that each of these advantages to foreign producers is ethically unfair, and so domestic industry should be protected from both export bounties and low wages abroad. Thus, in sum, in the absence of efficiency considerations, opinions about what "advantages" a foreign concern should be permitted to exercise in trade have varied. In reality, while it is possible to establish a set of rules by which the economy ought to operate so as to maximize social welfare, it is difficult to establish what is permissible on the grounds of business morality alone. The distinction between a "fair" and an "unfair" advantage has often been made simply to argue for tariff protection, and so it may well be in this instance.

Second, it is debatable that domestic firms should be protected from any advantage possessed by foreign rivals, whether artificial or natural, when the advantage results in permanently low-priced imports that increase economic welfare in the importing society. After all, the purpose of business is not to provide for the prosperity of any particular group of owners or workers, but to furnish society with the optimal bundle of consumer goods over time. The maintenance of economic liberties, such as the right to change jobs or to start a proprietorship, may be alternative moral goals for which it is worth sacrificing economic welfare. That it is worth foregoing a dependable supply of cheap imports on moral grounds because the exporter permanently prices below cost, however, is a decidedly more dubious proposition. In fact, it is one that import-competing producers are considerably more likely to view with favor than is the consuming public.

Nevertheless, it cannot be denied that the ethics of the above argument are a good deal more substantive than those previously attributed to Mr. Byrnes. Even in an era of trade liberalization, it might reasonably be maintained that domestic sellers should not be expected to compete with dumpers who price below cost. As has been discussed above, however, dumping does not indicate that an export price is or is likely to be below cost. It merely indicates that this possibility exists. Consequently, even if the morality embodied in the above argument is accepted, the correct procedure is not to prohibit dumping in itself, but to review instances of dumping and to sanction dumping when less-than-cost pricing actually occurs. Moreover, the penalty for such dumping should not be an additional duty equal to the dumping margin, as the present United States Antidumping Act requires, but a levy sufficient to raise the import price to the level of foreign unit cost. It may be argued in rebuttal that it is impossible to tell when a dumping price is above average total cost and when it is not and, therefore, that all dumping should be prohibited to preclude below-cost pricing. But it is difficult to see how such legislation could be expected to legitimately prevent unfair competition more often than it would unjustly prevent fair competition.

In summary, dumping cannot be condemned out of hand on the grounds that price discrimination in trade is inherently detrimental to the importing nation. Opponents of dumping have failed to show that dumping necessarily involves "unfair" import pricing. They have falsely argued that dumping results in tariff avoidance. And they have denounced dumping for causing injuries to the importing nation which occur with equal intensity and frequency under single pricing and for which restrictions on importation are an inappropriate remedy.

Moreover, although dumping permits foreign concerns to price exports below cost, dumping cannot be universally condemned on this basis either, for less-than-cost pricing will not customarily occur under normal economic conditions. And more importantly, from the standpoint of economic efficiency, less-than-cost pricing in itself does not injure the importing nation. Rather, it increases welfare therein by providing a supply of goods at a lower real cost than that which attaches to domestic production.

Furthermore, from an ethical point of view, less-than-cost pricing may run counter to the principle that a seller should not possess an illegitimate advantage in competition. But to preclude all dumping on this basis would probably require an inordinate sacrifice in welfare in the importing nation, and it would more than likely create an injustice to dumpers who price above cost as frequently as it mitigated unfair competition from pricing below cost.

Thus, on the whole, nations should not enact a blanket prohibition on dumping, as Canada has done.[b] If import dumping is to be properly regulated, governments should sanction the practice only in specific instances in which it can be shown to have a pernicious or unjust effect. We now turn to arguments that tender support for this type of legislation.

### The Case for Prohibiting Dumping That Injures Domestic Producers

While refusing to condemn all dumping, some critics of the practice have maintained that it should be prohibited whenever producers in the importing nation are injured. This recommendation is based on a single line of reasoning which emphasizes that dumping affords exporters an extraordinary amount of price flexibility.

The argument was first enunciated by F. W. Taussig, W. S. Culbertson, and J. Viner in the early 1900s, with its most extensive elaboration appearing in Viner's seminal work.[22] It has been continually repeated by modern-day commentators on the United States Antidumping Act, but their synopses have merely reiterated the case made by Viner et al., without critical evaluation of its validity.[23] The argument is of great importance to the legitimacy of our present antidumping law because it provides the most popular justification for sanctioning dumping that is not anticompetitive in effect on the grounds of economic efficiency.[c]

According to this argument, all temporarily cheap imports destabilize the import market and cause domestic producers to shift resources between industries, both at their advent and their cessation. As a result, resources are needlessly used up in shutting down and starting up domestic

---

[b] The Canadian law does not prohibit all dumping. It does, however, prohibit dumping whenever similar goods are made in Canada, without qualification as to the effect of the dumping on the domestic economy. *Antidumping and Countervailing Duties* (Geneva: General Agreement on Tariffs and Trade, 1958), pp. 55–58.

[c] The "temporary importation" argument described below is a slightly altered version of the case made by Viner in *Dumping: A Problem in International Trade* (chap. 8, see Endnote 22). Unless otherwise footnoted, the following discussion summarizes the opinion expressed by Viner therein.

operations. Output is lost because of transitory unemployment. Productivity diminishes because of the postponement of the maintenance and replacement of machinery and the deterioration of labor skills during layoffs. And growth is stymied by the retardation or termination of research and development projects. Thus, by generating an unproductive use of resources, factor unemployment, and productivity declines, impermanently cheap importation leads to a formidable loss of output to society.[d] In monetary form, this loss is largely born by producers and employees in the import-competing industry and by industries that use the cheap imports as inputs and whose prosperity is premised on the continual availability of the low-priced foreign supplies.

On the other hand, consumers of the imported article benefit to the extent that the temporary supply of cheap imports lowers prices during the interval in which it is forthcoming, and they lose over some succeeding period if prices are higher than otherwise because of the previous inflow of cheap foreign goods. Thus, while temporarily cheap importation always injures producers, it may raise or lower consumer welfare depending on whether the average price of obtaining the article over time is increased or reduced. In all probability, however, the net effect of temporarily inexpensive foreign supplies will be to lower consumer welfare originating in importables consumption or, at best, to raise it only slightly. To the degree that prices fall below normal during the period of importation, they will have to rise above customary levels in succeeding periods if normal profits are to be earned and a continuing flow of capital is to be attracted to the industry. Moreover, increased price variability in the downward direction will raise the risks accompanying import competition and thereby augment the rate of return needed to acquire capital.[e] Conse-

---

[d] Viner does not discuss the losses that domestic producers experience because of temporary importation. He merely asserts that such losses take the form of an injury to capital, labor, and managerial ability employed in the domestic industry and occur in substantial magnitude (Viner, pp. 137–44). Nevertheless, in discussing cyclical competition among domestic oligopolists, Scherer offers a number of reasons why producers may incur losses that affect society's welfare in adjusting to temporary downturns in demand, and Scherer's work is the origin of the above remarks. Frederick M. Scherer, *Industrial Market Structure and Economic Performance* (Chicago: Rand McNally and Co., 1970), pp. 200–201.

[e] Viner stated that consumers will benefit from dumping during the dumping interval because prices will be abnormally low. They will only receive a net benefit in the long run, however, if prices are not abnormally high after the dumping ceases. Viner proposed that consumers could lose from dumping, on balance, because of the threat of monopolization. He believed, however, that the risk of monopolization was too small to maintain that consumers would usually lose from dumping; and thus, if consumer interests alone were to be considered, dumping should be permitted (Viner, pp. 132–37).

It is, however, not necessary for the dumper to monopolize the import market for prices to be abnormally high after temporary dumping has occurred. One obvious reason for abnormally high prices other than monopolization is that a competitive industry will adjust in size

quently, the losses suffered by producers will outweigh any gains experienced by consumers. Thus, a case can be made for prohibiting all imports whose low price is transitory in nature whenever they injure a domestic industry.

On a case-by-case basis, however, it is generally impossible to discern whether a low import price is temporary or permanent. Consequently, the importation of inexpensive goods should be permitted unless the nature of the imports suggests that their low price will be short-lived. With respect to uniformly priced imports, the necessity of charging identical prices at home and abroad compels the firm to establish an export price that maximizes long-run profits because it leaves little room for temporary pricing strategies for other purposes. Thus, when imports are normally priced, the overwhelming probability is that the price will be of indefinite duration under stable market conditions.

We cannot assume that the dumper prices exports so as to maximize long-run profits, however, because dumping allows exporters to unilaterally reduce the price of foreign sales to achieve a number of short-run objectives. Thus, when dumping occurs, it may well be that import prices are inconstantly low. In fact, Viner asserts, even though it is possible for dumped imports to engender a permanently low price, characteristically their cheapness is only temporary. Hence, in any particular instance, the low price of dumped imports should be presumed to be a short-run phenomenon; and dumping that injures domestic industry to any degree should be prohibited because an injury on the supply side augurs a negative net change in society's welfare in spite of the benefits conferred on consumers of the dumped goods.

In summary, Viner's condemnation of dumping rests on two contentions. The first is that dumped imports characteristically engender a temporarily low price and therefore differ from ordinary imports. The second is that temporarily cheap imports which are harmful to domestic producers are also detrimental to society's economic well-being. In spite of the widespread and uncritical acceptance of Viner's argument, neither of these contentions is particularly meritorious.

---

so that a normal return on capital is earned in the long run. Thus, if subject to recurrent, transitory dumping, the number of firms in a competitive industry will eventually be such that the same average price is charged in the long run as that which would appear continuously in the absence of dumping. Consequently, prices will be abnormally high in nondumping periods to the same degree that they are abnormally low when dumping occurs, and consumer welfare will not change appreciably. Moreover, Sandmo has shown that the average price charged in competitive industries in which demand fluctuates will be greater than under conditions of constant demand if firms are risk averse. In addition, he speculates that unstable demand itself may lead to monopoly or oligopoly if some firms are risk neutral by discouraging production by risk-averse concerns. Thus, a modern restatement of Viner's theory must be a bit pessimistic about the effect of dumping on consumer welfare, in contrast to Viner's optimism. Agnar Sandmo "On ' the Theory of the Competitive Firm under Price Uncertainty," *American Economic Review* 61 (March 1971):65–73.

Concerning Viner's first contention, Robinson has shown that charging equal prices in two markets will only maximize a firm's profits if the demand curves therein have equal elasticities.[24] On this basis alone, one would expect competitors who can separate markets to regularly and continuously dump. Moreover, in Robinson's model, the incremental delivered cost of sales was the same for all markets because she only included production cost in her analysis. Simkin, however, has constructed a general-equilibrium model of price discrimination which includes marketing, distribution, and transportation costs. He has shown that price discrimination will evolve as a policy that maximizes long-run profits whenever marginal delivered costs differ between markets because of differences in the incremental expenses of selling, distributing, or transporting goods.[25] Thus, from a theoretical point of view, there is no a priori reason to label dumping a typically short-run pricing strategy. Rather, the theoretical work on dumping indicates that domestic monopolists who sell at home and abroad can be expected to continuously dump, except in rare instances in which a particularly fortuitous concatenation of demand and supply curves leads to uniform pricing.

Nevertheless, this does not rule out the possibility that, as an empirical matter, dumping, has been or is predominantly a short-run pricing strategy. In fact, it appears that Viner's observation on this score was derived empirically, for it preceded the marginalist analysis that revealed dumping to be a long-run, profit-maximizing strategy, except in anomalous circumstances. Furthermore, Viner drew his generalization from data that covered an era in which the manufacturers of Great Britain and, later, the syndicates of Germany and other nations were employing dumping as a short-run policy, mainly to relieve excess capacity in times of depression.[26] Thus, dumping may well have been primarily a temporary pricing policy in the century before 1923.

At the same time, however, there is reason to suspect that dumping is not equally as likely to be an impermanent policy today, for the structure and goals of the firm have changed radically since the early twentieth century. Prior to World War I, firms were primarily oriented toward their home market, and international trade was viewed as a source of residual sales: a source that could be turned to in times of depression. Reflecting this philosophy, sales departments were divided into domestic and international divisions, with the latter divisions decidedly secondary in status. Moreover, international markets were yet to be developed, and thus the problem of market entry was significant. In comparison, today the flow of trade has knitted nations together to such an extent that we have recently witnessed the emergence of the multinational enterprise. These and lesser concerns are not prejudiced in favor of domestic commerce but, rather, tend to think in terms of maximizing profits on a global basis, with sales in all nations of equal importance. As a result, marketing divisions are now distinguished by product type, with each division controlling both domestic and foreign sales.[27] And so too has the national identity of the corporation become a matter of little concern, with the result that the nation of incorporation is often chosen solely to minimize tax liabilities.[28] Thus, at present, the large enterprise, and even the medium-sized firm with a global viewpoint, is much more likely to dump as a permanent, profit-maximizing policy. Consequently, until some empirical evidence concerning the postwar period is provided, in spite of the preeminence of the source, the validity of Viner's statement that dumping is a short-run pricing policy is open to considerable doubt.

Moreover, this doubt is heightened by the fact that contrary to his assertions, Viner's study does not indicate that dumping will normally entail temporary price cutting under stable market conditions. As mentioned in Chapter 1, Viner's list of motives for dumping is the most exhaustive compiled to date. Yet, Viner sets forth only four motives for nonpredatory, intermittent dumping: (1) to gain entry into foreign markets; (2) to retaliate against dumping in the reverse direction; (3) to maintain connections in a market in which prices are, on remaining considerations, unacceptable; and (4) to maintain capacity utilization in times of domestic depression.[29] Of these motives, only "market entry" and "retaliation" will generate dumping in its pure gaming form, as temporary price cutting in the face of constant demand and supply parameters. Yet, these are not the kinds of goals that will lead to frequent or repetitive instances of underselling. Thus, by all appearances, Viner's contention that dumped imports are normally only temporarily cheap rests on the assumption that demand is inherently unstable.

With respect to the second plank in Viner's argument, the motives which he lists for transitory dumping in static equilibrium do not support the claim that such dumping will generally lower welfare in the importing country. Dumping done for retaliatory purposes will certainly produce a temporary supply of imports that will disrupt the market and injure domestic producers. Since the cheap imports will eventually be withdrawn, the injury on the supply side will not be offset by a permanent gain in consumer welfare, and thus, on a dynamic basis, dumping so motivated should be sanctioned. But dumping to gain market entry is entirely another matter, for, in this case, temporary dumping is not synonymous with a temporary supply of importables. Rather, to the extent that the foreign producer can attract customers by dumping, he will continue to supply them, if at a higher price in the future. Higher prices, of course, may chase some customers back to import-competing sellers, and thus to some extent an unnecessary movement of resources may take place. But the overriding effect of market entry will be to cause a once-and-for-all shift in resources away from the domestic production of importables, to increase competition in the import market, and to either lower the equilibrium price therein or furnish consumers with goods for which they are willing to pay a higher price on the basis of their tastes, the quality of the merchandise, or like considerations. Thus, in spite of the fact that some degree of temporary market disruption is a concomitant of market entry, short-run dumping for this purpose will enhance domestic welfare and should not be prohibited. In a fact, to do so would be to institute a potentially anticompetitive restriction on imports.

As for the last two motives for temporary dumping which Viner offers, it is of the utmost importance, in each case, that dumping occur in a state of economic disequilibrium and be a reaction to a fall in demand. Unlike the situation in which demand is constant, a temporary recession at home or abroad may induce a single pricer, as well as a dumper, to adjust export prices and sales on a short-run basis. Consequently, it remains to be seen whether dumping in response to an economic downturn creates a disturbance in the import market which differs from that forthcoming under single pricing. And it remains to be seen whether the difference between the two disturbances justifies the regulation of dumped imports alone.

Let us first consider a recession in the import market. It can be shown that if the object of pricing is strict profit-maximization, both a dumper and a single pricer will lower their export price and sales volume. However, in general, the dumper will tend to reduce the quantity of export sales by less and the price by more than will the single pricer.[30] Consequently, if the exporter is a short-run profit maximizer, the supply of imports will be less elastic if he is permitted to dump in response to a temporary downturn in demand than if he is not. When dumping is permitted, domestic concerns will be forced to bear a greater share of the burden of adjusting to recessions than they would otherwise incur. As a result, the flow of domestic resources between markets, involving as it does some transitory unemployment and other real costs, will be augmented.

Moreover, as Viner observes, dumping will permit the exporter to maintain foreign sales in order to retain continual contact with customers, even though the customary volume of exports can only be acquired at a price that reduces present profits. That dumping permits a nonprofit-maximizing response to recession abroad reinforces the tendency for the supply of imports to be less elastic than under normal importation. But, significantly, it does not create a distinction between dumped and normal imports additional to that which obtains when profit-maximizing behavior is assumed.

Consequently, even if allowance is made for nonprofit-maximizing behavior under dumping, we cannot recommend, as does Viner, that dumping in response to a recession abroad be prohibited because it causes market disruptions which would not otherwise occur. In point of fact, the market disturbance is due to the downturn in demand, and the only difference between the responses of the dumper and the single pricer to this downturn is that the dumper will withdraw from the market to a lesser degree. The sole basis for prohibiting temporary dumping during a recession in the import market, therefore, is that it will increase the transitory flow of resources between domestic industries. But this is not a sufficient basis for sanctioning short-run dumping. In the first place, the foreign goods are as permanent a source of supply as is domestic output, and there is no apparent reason why exporters who continually supply an import market in good faith should be forced to reduce sales in order to ameliorate the hardship experienced by native producers. In fact, such a policy might make foreign concerns reluctant to service the market, thereby lowering the welfare of the importing nation. Second, even if it should be deemed advisable to require exporters to forego sales to a specific degree when demand falls, a prohibition of dumping would not be the efficient or equitable way to achieve this goal. Rather, since the supply of imports may be inelastic even under single pricing, the proper legislation would make mandatory some specific reduction in all imports in a recessionary period. Such legislation would permit even unprofitable dumping to maintain trade connections as long as imports were reduced to the required degree, and it would prohibit importation under single pricing in excess of the legal amount.

With respect to a depression in the home market of the producer, if the firm continually exports under normal conditions, it will generally increase export sales regardless of whether or not dumping is permitted. If the firm prices so as to maximize short-run profits during the downturn, it can be shown that the rise in exports will tend to be less under dumping than single pricing. Thus, under strict profit-maximization, allowing dumping will ease the disturbance in the import market.[31] On the other hand, dumping makes feasible extensive price cutting in the export market at a sacrifice in present earnings for the purpose of simultaneously maintaining capacity output and a high home-market price. A firm may desire to engage in such a policy to avoid weakening its ability to charge a monopoly price in times of prosperity, to reduce the cost of temporary adjustments in plant utilization, or, as in the case of Japanese industry, to fulfill a social contract that makes the firm responsible for the welfare of its employees. Consequently, in spite of the salutary effect of profit-maximizing dumping, the net effect of the practice may well be to aggravate the disruption that necessarily occurs in the export market when home demand falls.

When the foreign producer does not normally engage in exportation, a depression in his home market is much more likely to induce him to export temporarily if he has the option of dumping. To reiterate, assuming profit maximization, Robinson's theory of price discrimination reveals that a dumper will begin to export when marginal revenue at the optimal volume of home sales in autarky becomes equal to the maximum nonzero-demand price abroad. For the single pricer, however, exportation only becomes profitable when domestic marginal revenue in autarky is far below this point, and thus home demand is much weaker. In addition, because dumping permits short-run, profit-sacrificing behavior, the dumper may begin to sell abroad to maintain capacity long before exportation becomes rewarding.

Moreover, whenever a domestic downturn would lead both a dumper and a single pricer to commence exportation, the volume of exports forthcoming and the consequent disturbance in the import market will most assuredly be greatest under dumping. As shown in Chapter 2, with few exceptions, a profit-maximizing dumper will export more than a profit-maximizing single pricer, and, again, the dumper may sell a greater amount of exports than is profitable to keep the home fires burning.

In summary with respect to dumping that arises from transient changes in demand in the producing nation, it can be argued that such dumping should be prohibited even though the firm normally engages in exportation. This position, however, is weak when the imports are regularly supplied, and the only harm attributable to the dumping is a possible intensification of the market disruption that would be forthcoming under a uniform price policy. On the other hand, a strong case can be made for prohibiting dumping when imports are not customarily marketed under normal demand conditions. In this instance, the importing nation does not receive continuous benefits from a persistent supply of goods, the ability to dump will often foster transitory importation that would not appear under single pricing, and it will always aggravate any market disturbance that would otherwise occur.

With respect to the overall validity of Viner's argument, given the multinational nature of production and distribution in the current world economy, it cannot be expected that dumping will generally, or even usually, involve temporary price cutting. Consequently, it cannot be said that dumping will normally create a transitory disruption in the import market, or that dumping which injures domestic producers will assuredly reduce welfare in the importing nation. Accordingly, legislation which prohibits all dumping that injures a domestic industry should not be enacted, for, in general, such legislation would prevent sustained dumping which augments competition and benefits the importing society.

Moreover, given the possible motives for short-run dumping, it cannot be assumed that such dumping will be accompanied by a temporary supply of imports whenever it occurs, since short-run dumping may be engaged in for the purpose of market entry or to maintain existing connections during a depression in the import market. In either of these instances, the exporter will continuously furnish a beneficial supply of imports in the future. Thus, there is no reason to restrict his ability to engage in price competition in a manner different from the limitations pertaining to domestic establishments. Consequently, even legislation prohibiting all temporary dumping is not justified by welfare considerations.

Nevertheless, dumping can lead to temporary exportation in some instances in which export sales would not be made under single pricing. Such exportation may occur to retaliate for the successful foreign-market penetration of American firms. It is likely to occur during a severe depression in the home market of foreign concerns, and it may take place in other circumstances. This type of dumping will, in fact, disrupt the import market and reduce welfare whenever it injures domestic producers. To this extent, Viner's argument possesses a grain of truth. Consequently, it is appropriate for nations to specifically prohibit dumping when it injures a domestic industry and, additionally, involves the importation of a temporary supply of goods which would not otherwise be marketed.

### The Case for Prohibiting Dumping That Has an Anticompetitive Effect on the Import Market

While the preceding argument provides one basis for regulating dumping, historically, the most important argument against the practice has been that it permits export price cutting for the purpose of monopolizing foreign markets. As indicated in Chapter 1, America's first antidumping statute was limited to preventing purposefully monopolistic dumping, and the fear of predatory market invasion by Germany provided the major impetus behind the United States Antidumping Act of 1921. When the efficiency of this law was questioned in the 1950s and 1960s, American industry's sole complaint was that the Act was inadequate to protect American markets from monopolization. In the main, those congressmen who supported a tightening of the Act's statutes at that time criticized the existing law for this reason.

Immediately after the American legislation was passed, Viner took exception to the popular notion that Germany had regularly dumped to destroy foreign competition, stating that German dumping was largely defensive.[32] With respect to the nature of dumping in recent decades, Seavy maintains that predatory dumping has not been in evidence since World War II,[33] and, in fact, only a few instances of predatory dumping have ever been documented. Thus, in the two periods in which protection against dumping has been an issue, it appears that those who pushed for strong antidumping legislation because of the imminent danger of predatory dumping may have overstated their case.

Nevertheless, in theory, it cannot be denied that dumping is considerably more amenable to predation than is single pricing. Predatory price cutting is best defined as the act of charging a lower price than is warranted by profit considerations alone in order to increase the monopoly power of the firm. The hallmark of the practice is the purposeful deviation of pricing behavior from that which is most profitable in the short run.[34] Its most malevolent form occurs when a large firm acquires a dominant share of the market by lowering prices until smaller or financially weaker firms are forced into bankruptcy. Less maliciously, the predator may cut prices to discipline his rivals and coerce them into complying with the price he sets, at a sacrifice in profits to themselves. When no competition exists, of course, predatory price cutting may still be employed to prevent entry into the industry and preserve the firm's monopoly position.

Since, fundamentally, it entails the sacrifice of present income for future gains, predatory price cutting in the market of exportation is properly viewed as an exercise of power via previous monopolization elsewhere. But the power to price aggressively abroad does not derive simply from the existence of monopoly at home, for power does not stem solely from a capacity to forego gains or survive losses. Rather, in the abstract, power is the ability to harm others while incurring only minor injuries oneself. One possesses or lacks power according as the ratio of the injury imposed on others to the cost incurred from an aggressive act is large or small. And, consequently, a monopolist will possess power in his export market only if he can adopt policies under which this ratio takes on a sufficiently large value.

Regardless of the degree of domestic monopoly, as long as a producer must charge identical prices at home and abroad, the full volume of his sales will be subject to the same low price that he imposes on his rivals. Thus, in the course of maximizing profits, a single pricer may monopolize a foreign market by charging a low price. But in most instances, he will lack the power to intentionally monopolize a market through price cutting; for, in order to undersell foreign competitors to an extent sufficient to bring about their demise, the firm will have to forego a substantial and, probably an intolerable, amount of present earnings. In contrast, dumping permits the producer to lower his price abroad while preserving high prices at home. Thus, only part of the dumper's sales are made at low prices while his rivals in the import market must reduce their price on all sales to maintain customers. Consequently, dumping increases the ratio of harm done to cost incurred and thereby bestows upon the firm the power of predatory market invasion.

From a narrow perspective, then, dumping permits the purposeful monopolization of import markets because it allows foreign concerns to price exports below their unit cost. Since such pricing behavior is precluded under single pricing, only the dumper can attempt to destroy competition in foreign markets when import-competing producers are more cost efficient. Moreover, from a broad perspective, when the foreign concern possesses a cost advantage over his rivals, predatory export pricing is still much more likely to occur under dumping than single pricing. In this situation, both a dumper and a single pricer may be able to force export prices to a level at which import-competing firms earn unacceptably low profits or even incur losses. But the dumper will be able to do so with a substantially smaller sacrifice in present earnings than that incurred by the single pricer, who is likely to be deterred from predatory market invasion by the riskiness of the venture and the magnitude of foregone profits required as an initial investment.

In general outline, the predatory argument against dumping is correct in asserting that dumping and single pricing differ because the former practice permits intentionally anticompetitive policies. Monopoly control of prices in its home market gives the firm a pool of excess profits that it can sacrifice in the interest of predatory gains abroad. Under single pricing, the link between home and export prices limits the firm's ability to price aggressively abroad by reducing the ratio of harm done to cost incurred to an intolerably small level. Under dumping, this linkage does not constrain the firm's selling behavior, and so it may reduce export prices specifically for the purpose of monopolizing the foreign market. On this basis, it is legitimate to restrict the purview of legislation aimed at prohibiting intentionally predatory import pricing to dumped imports.

This type of legislation is undesirable, however, simply because it could not be enforced: for there are insurmountable difficulties to proving intent on the part of the exporter to produce an anticompetitive effect in the import market. Accepting L. S. Keyes's criteria, stated above, that predatory intent can only be inferred when short-run profits are not being maximized, the determination of intent would necessitate a knowledge of both marginal revenue and marginal cost. Yet, it would probably be impossible for administrators to acquire the necessary cost data. Firms are not likely to be enthusiastic about revealing their costs to foreign governments. When exporters do tender cost information, the data may be falsified or, if accounting methods are markedly different abroad, the true cost of production may be easily disguised or hard to interpret. Moreover, firms that produce joint products or many different articles may not be able to calculate production costs for any one item.[f]

A more serious consideration is that even if accurate marginal or aver-

---

[f] Moreover, Clemens's analysis of the multiproduct firm indicates that such enterprieses can engage in predatory behavior identical to that which is permitted by dumping without running afoul of antidumping laws. Thus, antidumping legislation may be too narrow in scope to effectively remedy the problem of predatory market invasion due to temporary, profit-sacrificing exportation. Eli W. Clemens, "Price Discrimination and the Multiproduct Firm," *Review of Economic Studies* 19 (1950–51):1–11.

age cost data were available, marginal revenue in the import market would certainly be impossible to measure. Yet, predatory intent cannot be assessed by substituting the export price for marginal revenue and comparing it to marginal cost. Although one can deduce the existence of predatory intent with certainty when the export price is less than marginal cost, an absence of predatory intent cannot be inferred when it is greater. Moreover, predatory intent cannot be discerned by comparing the export price to average cost, as was suggested in a recent comment in the *Yale Law Journal;*[35] for profit maximization can occur at an export price below average total cost, while nonprofit maximization can occur when the export price exceeds unit cost.

In view of the difficulty of proving intent, the importing nation may wish to prohibit all dumping that is likely to have an anticompetitive effect on the structure of the market. Such a policy can be justified on the basis that it is geared to sanctioning purposefully anticompetitive pricing in the only way administratively feasible. At the same time, however, one cannot overlook the fact that antidumping legislation of this scope would represent a mandate against anticompetitive importation in itself. Since ordinary imports might also tend to reduce competition, especially when the exporter has a considerable cost advantage, the question arises as to why only dumped imports should be inspected for evidence of a tendency to monopolize. In this vein, it must be reiterated that a dumper will find less-than-cost export pricing to be profit maximizing whenever the elasticity of foreign demand exceeds the elasticity of his average total cost curve. As a result, a dumper is much more likely to price so as to injure competition, even without predatory intent, than is a single pricer. Because the possibilities of predatory pricing and less-than-cost pricing in the course of profit maximization only arise under dumping, the probability that cheap imports will adversely affect competition in the import market is substantially greater when dumping occurs. Accordingly, even if a reduction in competition in itself were deemed undesirable, it might be legitimate to enact legislation that requires an inspection of the effect of importation on the structure of competition only when dumping is extant.

## Conclusions

Our inspection of the case against dumping has revealed that it is not an abnormal pricing policy that differs markedly from single pricing. Rather, in a world in which demand elasticities and delivered costs differ between markets, exporters will usually dump in order to maximize long-run profits. Consequently, the price of dumped imports will customarily be a long-run price. The importation of dumped goods will normally enhance welfare, and nations should no more prohibit all dumping than they should prohibit all importation.

Moreover, although dumping may injure the importing nation in specific instances, this in itself does not justify the enactment of legislation to regulate the practice; for both single-priced and dumped imports will reduce welfare in a variety of circumstances. Accordingly some restrictions on importation in general are part and parcel of an optimal commercial policy. Additional statutes governing dumped imports alone are only warranted if dumping causes problems that do not occur or are unlikely to occur under single pricing, or are not alleviated by traditional import controls.

In this regard, it has been argued that dumping does not create an injury that cannot take place under uniform pricing, nor does it permit exporters to escape existing customs restrictions. However, it does significantly increase the danger that the importing nation will be harmed by either of two events whose occurrence is unlikely when imports are identically priced at home and abroad.

The first event is the monopolization of the import market by a foreign concern. Under single pricing, a foreign producer may monopolize the domestic market. He is unlikely to do so, however, because the need to maintain profits prevents him from reducing export prices temporarily in order to destroy competition, and forces him to price exports above average total cost in the long run. On the other hand, dumping permits a concern to price cut in selected export markets in the interest of predation. Moreover, when the dumper simply attempts to maximize profits, his long-run price will be less than average total cost whenever the elasticity of foreign demand exceeds the elasticity of his unit cost curve. Consequently, when dumping occurs, normal cost and profit considerations provide no protection against either an intended or unintended monopolization of the import market.

Second, welfare in the importing nation will be reduced whenever domestic producers are injured by a temporary influx of foreign goods. Temporary exportation may occur under single pricing because uniform pricers may well turn to foreign markets for sales in the event of a severe depression at home. Given an opportunity to dump, however, it is much more likely that producers will resort to foreign sales to maintain production in times of depression; in addition, producers who dump can engage in temporary export sales for other reasons. Thus, in this respect also, dumping does not cause an injury that is precluded by single pricing, but it greatly enhances the probability that the injury will take place.

For these reasons then legislation aimed at regulating dumping is called for. Such legislation should not prohibit all dumping; it should merely employ dumping as a signal that sufficient danger of either of the above events exists to warrant further investigation into the effect of the imports. Moreover, when used as a signal, dumping should not be defined as the pricing of exports below that charged in the producer's home market (in accordance with the economist's construction of the term), because it is not this price differential that raises the possibility of predatory price cutting, pricing below cost, or temporary exportation. Rather, in a world in which producers may market output on a global basis, it is the pricing of exports below the average return presently earned in all markets normally supplied by the foreign concern that forewarns of this phenomenon. Thus, antidumping laws should require an investigation into the effects of import sales whenever import prices fall short of the average return to the producer in other markets in which he customarily sells.

In addition, to prevent a protectionist application, such laws should specify that dumping should only be penalized if it reduces or is likely to reduce competition in the import market, or if it is accompanied by a temporary supply of imports that injures domestic concerns. In this respect, it is immediately apparent that the wording of the United States Antidumping Act is entirely too ambiguous. The Act merely directs the ITC to determine whether "an industry in the United States is being or is likely to be injured, or prevented from being established" because of foreign dumping. Since the Act does not define the meaning of injury, the ITC can construe injury to mean simply a significant harm to domestic producers. If it does so, dumping will be prohibited when it is neither anticompetitive in effect nor temporary in duration, and domestic producers will be protected at the expense of the commonweal. On the other hand, the merit of the definition of dumping employed under the Act is less obvious, and so it is to this topic that our attention now turns.

### Endnotes

1. Joan Robinson, *The Economics of Imperfect Competition* (London: Macmillan and Co., Ltd., 1933), p. 181.

2. C. G. F. Simkin, "Some Aspects and Generalizations of the Theory of Discrimination," *Review of Economic Studies* 15 (1947–48):1–13.

3. Tibor de Scitovsky, "A Reconsideration of the Theory of Tariffs," *Review of Economic Studies* 9 (Summer 1942): 89–110.

4. Charles P. Kindleberger, *International Economics,* 3d ed. (Homewood, Ill.: Richard D. Irwin, Inc., 1963), pp. 220–22.

5. Wolfgang F. Stolper and Paul A. Samuelson, "Protection and Real Wages," *Review of Economic Studies* 9 (November 1941):58–73.

6. See U.S., Congress, House, remarks of Mr. Collier, 88th Cong., 2d sess., 14 April 1964, *Congressional Record* 110:7842; and U.S., Con-

gress, Senate, remarks of Senator Scott, 89th Cong., 1st sess., 26 May 1965, *Congressional Record* 111:11809.

7. Bart S. Fisher, "The Antidumping Law of the United States: A Legal and Economic Analysis," *Law and Policy in International Business* 5 (1973):145–47.

8. U.S., Congress, House, Committee on Ways and Means, *Tariff Hearings, Undervaluation and Antidumping Duties, Hearings Before a Subcommittee of the House Committee on Ways and Means.* VI, 62d Cong., 3d sess., 1913, pp. 6149–50.

9. U.S., Congress, House, 85th Cong., 1st sess., 29 August 1957, *Congressional Record* 103:16522.

10. R. A. Anthony, "The American Response to Dumping from Capitalist and Socialist Countries; Substantive Premises and Restructured Procedures after the 1967 GATT Code," *Cornell Law Review* 54 (January 1969):159–231.

11. Ibid., pp. 164–65.

12. Ibid., pp. 168–70.

13. Ibid., pp. 170–71.

14. Ibid., p. 171.

15. Ibid., pp. 171–72.

16. Ibid., pp. 172–74.

17. Ibid., p. 174.

18. Ibid., p. 175.

19. Ibid., p. 177.

20. A. A. Walters, "Production and Cost Functions," *Econometrica* 31 (January 1963):1–66.

21. See W. M. Curtiss, *The Tariff Idea* (New York: The Foundation for Economic Education, Inc., 1953), pp. 56–60.

22. See Jacob Viner, *Dumping: A Problem in International Trade* (Chicago: University of Chicago Press, 1923), chap. 8; F. W. Taussig, *Some Aspects of the Tariff Question,* 3d ed. (Cambridge: Harvard University Press, 1931), pp. 203–206; and William Smith Culbertson, *Commercial Policy in Wartime and After* (New York: D. Appleton and Co., 1919), chap. 8.

23. See Peter D. Ehrenhaft, "Protection Against International Price Discrimination: United States Countervailing and Antidumping Duties," *Columbia Law Review* 58 (1958):47, n. 19. The reader should note how Ehrenhaft misinterprets Viner's discussion to reinforce the point that he wishes to make by omitting the nonpredatory motives for intermittent dumping listed by Viner; James A. Kohn, "The Antidumping Act: Its Administration and Place in American Trade Policy," *Michigan Law Review* 60 (February 1962):410–11; and James Keith Weeks, "Introduction to the Antidumping Law: A Form of Protection for the American Manufacturer," *Albany Law Review* 35 (1970–71):182–83, n. 7.

24. Robinson, p. 181.

25. Simkin, pp. 1–13.

26. Viner, pp. 35–94.

27. For a summary of the organizational changes that occur during the global expansion of a firm, see Sanford Rose, "The Rewarding Strategies of Multinationalism," *Fortune* 78 (September 1968):101–105.

28. For a discussion of transfer pricing by multinationals in attempting to maximize profits that includes a section on dumping, see L. W. Copithorne, "International Corporate Transfer Prices and Government Policy," *Canadian Journal of Economics* 4 (August 1971).

29. Viner, pp. 23–31.

30. William A. Wares, "An Evaluation of the Provisions and Recent Administrative History of the United States Antidumping Act of 1921" (Ph.D. diss., University of Michigan, 1976), Appendix.

31. Ibid.

32. Viner, pp. 61–66.

33. William Arthur Seavy, *Dumping since the War; The GATT and National Laws* (Oakland: Office Services Corp., 1970), pp. 2–3.

34. Lucile Sheppard Keyes, "Price Discrimination in Law and Economics," *Southern Economic Journal* 27 (April 1961):320–28.

35. "Comment—The Antidumping Act; Tariff or Antitrust Law?" *Yale Law Journal* 74 (1965):707–24.

# 4 | The Appraisal of Dumping in American Antidumping Proceedings

The definition of dumping employed in American antidumping proceedings has arisen partly from the provisions of the Antidumping Act and partly from procedures for calculating price differentials established by the Treasury Department. The definition stood unaltered from 1921 until the 1950s, however, in recent decades it has been reformed both by amendments to the Act and changes in Treasury Department practice. The method by which antidumping duties are calculated, is specified in the Act and it also has undergone some recent revisions.

In this chapter, the definition of dumping utilized in American proceedings and the magnitude of remedial duties mandated by the Act are evaluated. The chapter is divided into two sections. The first describes the American definition of dumping; the second appraises this definition in the light of the guidelines for optimal antidumping legislation derived in Chapter 3.

## The Definition of Dumping and the Dumping Margin under the United States Antidumping Act

Determination of the existence of dumping and the amount of the dumping margin involves a comparison between the price of sales to the United States and a standard of the foreign value of the merchandise. Under the Antidumping Act, this comparison is made on a net FOB factory basis.

### Calculation of the American Import Price

From its inception, the Antidumping Act contained detailed instructions for computing the FOB factory price of sales to the United States, and its directives have changed little since 1921.[1]

When the importer and exporter are unrelated, the Act defines the United States import price as the "purchase price." According to the Act, the purchase price is calculated by taking the price at which the American importer purchased or agreed to purchase the merchandise and adding the following items: (1) any costs of packaging and readying the goods for shipment to the United States not previously included therein;

(2) any import duties rebated by the exporting country because of the exportation of the merchandise; (3) any direct taxes rebated by the exporting country, to the extent that such taxes are normally included in prices on home sales; and (4) any rebated taxes whose noncollection constitutes an export bounty.[2]

The first of these additions is made to arrive at the FOB factory price of the imports in a condition ready for shipment to the United States, and a similar sum is included in the foreign values used to judge American import prices. Direct taxes and import duties are added to the sales price, if omitted therefrom, because rebating these levies upon exportation is permissible and should not result in findings of dumping. Of course, the granting of export bounties is not acceptable practice. But export bounties are included in the purchase price because dumping that arises from such subsidies falls within the purview of United States countervailing duty legislation, and not the Antidumping Act. Furthermore, when merchandise is sold to an importer CIF, the sales price must be adjusted to reduce it to the FOB factory level. According to the Act, the necessary subtractions are any export taxes and any expenses of delivering the goods to their destination in the United States which were included in the price to the importer.[3]

If the importer is an agent, consignee, or subsidiary of the exporter, or is otherwise related to him, the Act indicates that the "exporter's sales price" is the appropriate measure of the price of sales to the United States. The basis for computing the exporters sale's price is the price at which the importing concern resells the merchandise in the American marketplace. This price is transformed into the desired net FOB factory price through the same additions and subtractions used to calculate the purchase price, with two differences. First, in adjusting for the fact that the importer's resale price is the CIF price of the exports, in addition to the usual subtractions, the amount of commissions and of selling expenses incurred for the account of the exporter are deducted from the resale price. Second, if the exported merchandise was subjected to further processing or assembly in the United States before resale, any increased value stemming therefrom is subtracted in arriving at the exporter's sales price.[4]

### Calculation of the Foreign Values of American Imports

The procedures used to calculate the net FOB factory price of American imports are quite simple and are precise enough to reduce the Treasury Department's computations to a mathematical exercise involving little, if any, discretion. The process for assessing the foreign value of imports outlined by the Act is at once more complex and more ambiguous. To some extent, the complexity and generality of the definition of foreign value are inherent in the concept itself, involving, as it does, the estimation of a general price level rather than the adjustment of a specific set of prices to an FOB factory basis.

On the other hand, the circumstances surrounding the foreign transactions on which a standard of foreign value is based often differ from those surrounding the importation of goods into the United States in a manner that alters the seller's costs or the value of the merchandise. In either instance, the American import price may legitimately differ from prices charged on other transactions, and dumping or its absence cannot be inferred from a naive price comparison. Rather, allowances have to be made for differences in the details concerning the two transactions, either in estimating the relevant United States sales price or the foreign value. Under the Antidumping Act, such allowances are to be made in calculating the foreign value, although they could well have been introduced in the definition of the import price to the United States. As a result, the mathematical simplicity of the definitions of purchase price and exporter's sales price is preserved while the calculation of foreign values involves the Treasury Department in a substantial amount of decision making.

The Antidumping Act defines three standards of value to which the purchase price or exporter's sales price is to be compared by the Secretary of the Treasury. In calculating the dumping margin for the purpose of assessing antidumping duties, the American selling price is to be compared to the "foreign market value" of the merchandise or, in its absence, the "constructed value."[5] In determining the existence or absence of dumping, the relevant standard of comparison is the import's "fair value."[6] While the Act offers extensive instructions on the calculation of foreign market value and constructed value, it does not describe the term "fair value" other than to say that it is the appropriate measure for finding dumping. Consequently, the interpretation of fair value is left entirely to the Secretary.

From 1921 to 1955, the Secretary of the Treasury construed the fair value of imports as their foreign market value or constructed value, as defined in the Act. Moreover, little attention was paid to the manner in which an import's fair value was calculated during this period because the Secretary was responsible for deciding both whether dumping was occurring and whether an American industry was being injured thereby. Treasury Department practice was to consider the issue of injury first, delaying a serious inquiry into the question of dumping until a harmful effect was discovered, and so it disposed of many antidumping cases without having to make problematic price comparisons.[7]

In 1954 an amendment to the Antidumping Act placed the determination of injury in the hands of the International Trade Commission and stipulated that the injury issue was not to be addressed until dumping was found.[8] As a result, the Treasury Department decided to refine the manner in which fair value was assessed, and the method for its calculation that emerged from the Treasury's reforms differed substantially from that outlined by the Antidumping Act for computing an import's foreign-market value.[9] The two terms remained conceptually identical, however; and the disparities in their computation were erased in 1958, when the Act was amended to incorporate the Treasury's procedures.[10] Additional changes in the Treasury's procedures for calculating fair value took place in the 1960s and early 1970s, but these elaborated on the definition of foreign-market value contained in the Act and were applied in its calculation as well.[11] Thus, in sum, the fair value standard for deciding the dumping issue has undergone significant revisions in recent decades. Nevertheless, although the term "fair value" suggests that an ethical judgment might be involved in finding dumping, the Secretary of the Treasury has abjured such considerations and has continually interpreted fair value to be equivalent to a good's foreign-market value, as defined in the Antidumping Act.

According to the Act, the primary measure of an import's foreign-market value is its home-country price. As defined therein, this is the price, as of the date of exportation, at which such or similar merchandise is sold or offered for sale in the principal markets of the exporting country in the usual wholesale quantities, in the ordinary course of trade, for home consumption; plus all costs of readying the goods for shipment to the United States, if not included in that price. The subsidiary measure of foreign-market value described in the Act is the price at which the relevant merchandise is sold, in like manner, for export to countries other than the United States.[12] And an import's constructed value is the sum of four items: (1) the cost of materials and fabrication at a time far enough in advance of the date of exportation of the merchandise to permit its production; (2) the amount of general expenses usually incurred by producers of such merchandise in the country of exportation, not to be less than 10% of direct costs; (3) the amount of profits normally made by such producers, not to be less than 8% of all costs; and (4) any additional costs of readying the goods for shipment to United States markets.[13]

In accordance with the Act's instructions, the Secretary of the Treasury calculates foreign-market values by referring to the home-country price of imports on the date of purchase or agreement to purchase, whenever this precedes the exportation date. He customarily uses the home-market price as the basis for appraising an import's foreign-market value, and turns to third-country prices only when comparable merchandise is not sold in the exporting country or sales for home consumption are too small a percentage of all non-United States sales to furnish an adequate basis for comparison.[14] In this respect, present Treasury Department practice is to employ the home-country price in measuring foreign-market values unless home sales are less than 5% of all non-United States sales.[15] Finally, the Secretary bases his estimate of an import's foreign value on its constructed value, rather than its foreign-market value, whenever home and third-country prices cannot be determined.[a]

In addition, in the past the Treasury Department often found it impossible to estimate the fair or foreign-market value of imports from state-controlled economies by any of the methods prescribed by the Act. Under the prevailing philosophy, the home-market price could not be used as a basis for these values because there was no assurance that this price evolved from the forces of supply and demand rather than government manipulation. The price of exports to third countries was potentially a dumping price and therefore unacceptable. And the data needed to calculate constructed values usually could not be obtained. Consequently, the Treasury established the practice of basing fair value and foreign-market value on the price charged by a comparable free-market economy on the sale of similar merchandise either for home consumption or for export to all markets, including the United States.[16] Furthermore, in the Trade Act of 1974, Congress amended the statutory definition of foreign-market value to include this method of calculating the term in the case of imports from state-controlled economies.[17]

Once the Secretary of the Treasury has selected the proper measure of an import's foreign-market value, he adjusts this figure to account for differences in the circumstances that surround foreign transactions and United States sales. If the merchandise sold for home consumption or for export to third-party nations differs from the American imports, or if purchasers outside of the United States are restricted as to their use of the merchandise, he adjusts his estimate of foreign-market value to the extent that the differences or restrictions on use alter the value of the goods.[18]

The Secretary of the Treasury will also adjust his estimate of foreign-market value when merchandise is sold to the United States in different quantities from those involved in foreign transactions. Sales to the United States often involve larger quantities than home-market sales, however, and in the past American industry complained that the Treasury Department's practice of freely granting allowances for quantity discounts unfairly permitted foreign concerns to escape antidumping prosecution. Consequently, to discourage exporters from claiming exorbitant allowances for quantity discounts, present Treasury policy is to refuse to

---

[a] The Act provides that constructed values should be used in lieu of foreign-market values in some other instances as well, but this is the general rule that is followed by the Secretary. *Antidumping Regulations, Code of Federal Regulations,* Title 19, sec. 153.5 (1975).

reduce its estimate of foreign-market values to account for such discounts unless one of two conditions is satisfied: either the discounts are justified by cost savings on large-lot sales, or discounts of the same magnitude have been given on at least 20% of home (or third-country) sales in the six months preceding the antidumping complaint.[19]

Finally, in arriving at an import's foreign-market value, the Secretary of the Treasury makes allowance for other differences in circumstances of sale, provided that such differences bear a direct relationship to the sales involved. Thus, according to Treasury Department regulations, the home (or third-country) price may be adjusted for differences in credit terms, guarantees, warranties, technical assistance, servicing, advertising and other selling costs, and commissions pertaining to home sales and sales for export to the United States.[20] But the Secretary will probably not alter the foreign-market value of imports because the bad-debt ratio on home-market sales differs from that accompanying sales to American concerns.[21]

In order to judge whether dumping is occurring, then, the Secretary of the Treasury has had to make three broad decisions. First, he has had to choose a conceptual standard by which to evaluate American import prices and has opted for the concept of foreign-market value contained in the Antidumping Act. Second, he has had to select a basic measure of this standard, and, in accordance with the Act, he has given primacy to the home-market price. Third, he has had to promulgate rules for adjusting this measure when differing circumstances of sale rule out a direct comparision between the home-market price and import prices, and he has done so in the manner described above. In the remainder of this chapter, each of these aspects of present policy regarding dumping is appraised.

## An Evaluation of the Definition of Dumping and the Determination of Antidumping Duties

### General Concept of Fair Value

The broadest issue that has arisen concerning the determination of dumping in American proceedings is the correct interpretation of the term "fair value." Throughout the history of antidumping investigations, the Treasury Department has consistently equated the fair value of imports to their foreign-market value, as described in the Antidumping Act. This definition was not rigorously adhered to in the period 1955 to 1958. But even in this brief time, the Treasury deviated from it only in minor respects, not because of a belief that fair value and foreign-market value should be dissimilar, but merely because a slightly different construction of fair value facilitated the Act's administration.

Moreover, the Treasury Department's position on the meaning of fair value has had considerable support. At the time of the law's enactment, Viner asserted that foreign-market value, as defined by the Act, was the correct concept to be used in discerning dumping because the term was so defined that a comparison between it and the sales price of goods to the United States would reveal dumping only in cases that fit the economist's definition of the practice.[22] In cases of exchange dumping and surplus dumping (or in instances in which other types of spurious dumping existed), there would be no difference between an import's foreign-market value, computed via the Act's dictates, and its price in importation. The practice of equating fair value and foreign-market value has also been praised on the grounds that it is administratively efficient and that it minimizes any uncertainty concerning the comparison made by the Treasury in finding dumping. And, in *Kleberg and Co., Inc.* v. *the U.S.*, the Court of Customs and Patent Appeals found foreign-market value to be the most reasonable interpretation of fair value.[23]

Nevertheless, some commentators on the Act have objected to the "mathematical test" of dumping that arises when fair value is construed as foreign-market value. For example, P. D. Ehrenhaft and J. A. Kohn have maintained that the legislative history of the Act suggests that Congress did not intend fair value and foreign-market value to be equivalent.[24] Initially, their argument goes, the House antidumping bill contained only the term "foreign home value" (equivalent to the term "foreign market value" contained in the final version of the Act) as the standard to be used both in discovering dumping and in calculating antidumping duties. Thus, the House anticipated the employment of a mathematical test of dumping, reflecting the economic meaning of the term, to be carried out by customs appraisers. The Senate, however, wanted some higher-level consideration, so it rewrote the antidumping bill and placed the final decision on dumping in the hands of the Secretary of the Treasury. While retaining the mathematical test of foreign-home value for applying antidumping duties, the Senate directed the Secretary to find dumping by comparing the import price to a good's fair value. In leaving fair value undefined, the Senate intended that the Secretary would use his discretion in finding dumping and would investigate "why the purchase price was at its present level." Hence, Congress did not intend dumping, under the Act, to be equivalent to the economist's definition of the term, nor that it should be discovered through an inflexible test.[25] In fact, Ehrenhaft feels it would have been inconceivable for Congress to assign to the Secretary the task of finding dumping if it merely involved carrying out the calculation of foreign-market value that was rigidly specified in the Act.[26]

How, then, should the Secretary of the Treasury define fair value? According to Kohn, the answer is implicit in the legislative discussions conducted during the Act's term in Congress. Congress repeatedly emphasized that the Act was intended to fight "unfair competition," and thus it is in this context that the term fair value should be construed. Accordingly, in initiating antidumping proceedings, the Secretary should attempt to discover whether imports are being sold at a price below the competitive level and should interpret fair value as a standard of the competitive value of the goods in American markets. As Kohn succinctly put it, the test for dumping should be a "competitive price test."[27]

In spite of the logic of Kohn's argument, however, in the last analysis the "competitive-price-test" formulation of fair value is unacceptable. From both historical and policymaking points of view, there are stronger reasons for believing that Congress did intend fair value to mean foreign-market value.

With respect to the legislative history of the Act, it is true that the House bill offered only the foreign-market-value standard for determining both the existence of dumping and the dumping margin. In addition, however, the House bill directed the customs appraisers to ascertain the foreign-market value of all imports, to check for dumping on all imports, and to levy antidumping duties whenever dumping was found.[28] And in the explanatory report to its antidumping bill, the Senate did not object to the use of foreign-market value in determining dumping. Rather, the report argued that the House proposal placed inordinate responsibility for levying a tarifflike duty in the hands of minor officials, that searching for dumping on all imports would unreasonably burden the Customs Service, and that it was wrong to subject all dumped imports to additional duties without regard to their effect in the American marketplace.

The report stated that to remedy the first two inadequacies of the House bill, the Senate proposal placed responsibility for determining dumping in the hands of the Secretary of the Treasury. In order to rectify the third inadequacy, the Senate measure required the Secretary to decide whether dumped imports were injuring a domestic industry before levying additional duties.[29] This task, handed the Secretary along with the duty of finding dumping, involves a great deal of judgment, both with respect to deciding if an injury exists and if it is caused by the dumped imports. Moreover, from the preceding description of foreign-market value, as defined by the Act, it is apparent that the practical application of this term engenders a substantial amount of discretionary decision making so that even in equating fair value to foreign-market value, the duties of the Secretary in finding dumping are by no means perfunctory. Thus, it is not necessary to assume that the Senate intended the Secretary to use his discretion in interpreting fair value in order to explain why the Senate engaged him in the antidumping process. In fact, such an assumption is highly speculative, receiving no support from the Senate report or from the hearings that produced the objections to the House bill voiced therein.

The logic of the Act as an instrument of commercial policy also suggests that Congress intended fair value to mean foreign-market value, and certainly not "the competitive price of imports" in any case. For the Act stipulates that antidumping duties are warranted only if an American industry is injured "by reason of" imports that are dumped. Since it is mainly through price cutting that dumped imports can be expected to create the requisite injury, the issue of causation itself necessarily involves consideration of whether or not the import price is less than a competitive price. It would be strange if Congress had directed the Treasury Department to inquire into whether imports were priced at less than a competitive level and also to ask if there was an injury "by reason of" the dumped imports; for under such instructions, the clause "by reason of" would largely be redundant.

Rather, from the congressional discussions, it appears that Congress viewed dumping, in the economic sense, as potentially predatory in intent. Since experience with the 1916 Revenue Act had demonstrated that a showing of intent could not be required in a functional antidumping statute, Congress dropped this prerequisite to prosecution. But dumping was retained as the signal that anticompetitive sales were potentially taking place. In the Antidumping Act of 1921, Congress instructed the Secretary of the Treasury to look for this signal by comparing a good's import price to its foreign value. And only when the signal light was on and there was a threat to the domestic economy was he to levy additional duties.

Moreover, the rationale behind antidumping legislation discussed in Chapter 3 indicates that, in general, the Act's definition of foreign-market value is the correct measure to be used in initiating antidumping proceedings. To reiterate, in attempting to protect the import market from destabilization and monopoly control, the case for regulating dumped, rather than all, imports is that a single-price seller incurs the same average profit or loss on sales in all markets. Thus, his ability to price cut in any one market for short-run or predatory reasons is sharply limited by the angst of equity and debt holders and by his average total cost curve. The dumper, however, earns greater than average revenue in markets other than the one dumped on. And he may thus maintain acceptable profits while selling at a low rate of return or even a loss in a particular export market. Consequently, an extraordinary threat to the import market is caused by the deviation of the import price from the firm's average earnings in other markets, and it is the existence of such a deviation that properly serves to indicate that the effect of the imports in question merits review. The appropriate interpretation of fair value within the context of antidumping legislation is the average revenue normally earned by the exporting concern on non-United States sales at the time of purchase by the American importer. For the most part, the Act's definition of foreign-market value reflects such earnings, as Congress intended it should; and thus, by and large, it is an acceptable measure of fair value.

Nevertheless, the definition of foreign-market value originally contained in the Act had a number of shortcomings which made it a somewhat inaccurate measure of an exporter's average earnings on non-United States sales. Apparently because of these deficiencies the Treasury Department deviated from its unqualified use of foreign-market value as a standard of fair value in 1955, and the Act was subsequently amended in 1958 to incorporate the Treasury's reforms. Thus, there has been some parallel evolution in the construction of both fair value and foreign-market value. On the whole, however, in the course of this evolution the Treasury's interpretation of fair value has not been ideal, nor is it at present.

*Errors in the Calculation and Application of Foreign Market Value*

As mentioned above, the Treasury Department normally relies exclusively on the home-market price of imports in calculating their fair value, and only uses the price charged on exports to third-party nations when sales for home consumption are less than 5% of all non-United States sales. Thus, one serious flaw in the Treasury's definition of fair value is that it assigns undue importance to home-market prices in the exporting nation. Given the rationale for antidumping legislation, the relevant question to be posed before initiating an antidumping inquiry is, does the average revenue earned on non-United States sales suggest that the exporter is sacrificing profits (or incurring losses) in order to sell in the United States? When the firm exports only to the United States, or other export markets are entirely insignificant, an assessment of the home price alone may provide an answer to this question. But when third-country purchases are an important element in the firm's sales, it may often be the case that a proper answer cannot be arrived at without considering prices thereon, even if home sales predominate.

Consider, for example, the case in which 70% of all non-United States sales are made at home during the period of alleged dumping at a price of $10, and 30% are exported sales at an average price of $7. Is this concern dumping in the United States if it charges $9 in the American marketplace? Relying on the home-market price alone, the answer is unambiguously yes. And, in fact, it may be correct procedure to consider only the home-market price, for the volume of sales to the United States may be so large relative to other export sales that home sales are clearly the only alternative to exportation to American markets. Or the foreign concern may have just begun to sell to third-party nations on a sporadic or short-run basis, so that third-market prices are not indicative of the price normally obtained by the exporter.

But suppose that sales to the United States are only 10% of total sales and, therefore, only one-fourth of all export sales. And suppose that the exporting country has a history of selling abroad at the $7 price. Can we simply compare the American selling price to the home price and conclude that dumping exists? Is this dumping, so defined, grounds for beginning an antidumping investigation when, by grounds for such a proceeding, we mean that the exporter appears to be foregoing more profitable sales to dispose of goods in the United States at low prices? Or should we say that domestic monopoly in the country of origin, together with a history of sales in third markets at prices lower than the United States import price, makes the American selling price acceptable within the meaning of the Antidumping Act?

The answer, of course, is a matter of judgment. Giving primacy to the home-market price permits the administering agency to avoid exercising such judgment. It also makes the findings of such agencies appear definitive. But, clearly, it does not necessarily furnish a rational basis for beginning an antidumping investigation and, in fact, encourages investigations that are theoretically groundless.

Similarly, from the above discussion it is apparent that the Treasury Department should not calculate constructed value precisely according to the Act's provisions when it is to serve as a standard of fair value. The discussion of the constructed value in the Senate hearings indicates that this concept was included in the Act as a measure of last resort, inferior to foreign-market value calculated by either method because of the difficulty of acquiring accurate cost data. This same problem apparently induced Congress to require that constructed value include general expenses amounting to no less than 10% of direct costs and profits of at least 8% of all costs.[30] It would have been better, however, to direct the Secretary of the Treasury to abide by these lower limits only when he suspected that representations as to customary costs and profits made by producers in the exporting country were false. In calculating fair value as constructed value, rigid adherence to these lower limits—when it appears that producers are correct in claiming a lower rate of profits and indirect costs per unit of sales—will only create an inordinately high estimate of the customary average return. As a consequence, antidumping investigations may be commenced in situations in which they are inappropriate.

Neither of the above anomalies concerning the base price from which fair value is estimated has received much attention from critics of the Antidumping Act. One subject that has been discussed is the Treasury Department's method of calculating fair value in the case of imports from state-controlled economies. As previously mentioned, in these cases, Treasury practice is to reject the home and third-country export prices of the goods in question and to turn to the price charged by a similar free-market economy on the sale of like merchandise at home or in export to other nations, including the United States. As other authors have pointed out, the rationale for this policy is that prices in state-controlled economies are determined by macroeconomic forces. That is, they are ration prices set in accordance with an overall economic plan and, therefore, are not necessarily influenced by cost and profit considerations. Export prices in turn are set to acquire a volume of foreign exchange sufficient to obtain the imports required in the economic plan and may thus be dumping prices themselves.

According to Styne, Anthony, and P. B. Feller, the merit of this aspect of Treasury Department policy and the validity of its underlying rationale are somewhat questionable.[31] On the latter score, Anthony argues that there is no reason to summarily reject the home price in state-controlled economies as a basis for fair value, nor is it logical to blindly accept this price in cases of alleged dumping by free-market economies; for free-market economies contain some government-imposed controls, while not all controls affect domestic prices so as to render them meaningless. Thus, with respect to imports from either type of economy, the Treasury should inquire into whether the nature of existing controls makes the home price inadequate as a standard of fair value.[32]

On the other hand, Feller does not question the Treasury Department's rejection of the home price in Eastern-bloc nations, but he maintains that the price of goods in export to free-market economies cannot be summarily dismissed. While command economies control both parties to a domestic transaction, he observes, the buyer in East-West trade is a free agent interested in purchasing at the lowest price. Furthermore, command economies are generally interested in maximizing their hard-currency earnings, and, as a result, they attempt to sell in the West at the highest obtainable prices. Consequently, the free-market price of Eastern-bloc goods is competitively determined and may serve as their fair value.[33]

Moreover, Feller continues, the present procedure used by the Treasury Department in determining dumping has a number of shortcomings. When it bases fair value on the price of goods exported by a Western country to the United States and elsewhere, the Treasury may be relying on prices which are themselves the outcome of dumping. It would have no way of knowing this, however, unless an antidumping complaint had been filed against the exporter. The articles produced by a similar free-market economy and therefore used in the fair value determination, may not be reasonably comparable to the corresponding manufactures of the state-controlled economy. And it may be impossible to accurately adjust the free-market price for structural differences between the free and command economies. Thus, with respect to imports from Eastern-bloc countries, some other measure of fair value is called for.[34]

While the above criticisms raise some valid points, their condemnation of present Treasury Department practice is entirely too severe. Regarding Anthony's observations, the perfunctory rejection of the home-market price would be an error if it were possible to devise a general test of whether or not this price is affected by government controls. Anthony feels that such a test can be constructed. He recommends that the Treasury compare the home price of the imports in question to the home prices of a representative market basket of goods consumed in the exporting country. If the price ratio is the same as that found in Western economies, controls in the command economy have not distorted the home price in a manner that makes it unacceptable as a measure of fair value.[35]

This test, however, is obviously faulty, for it assumes that cost and demand conditions would equate relative prices in all economies were it not for the existence of internal controls. While this outcome is imaginable under a specific set of conditions, trade theorists have shown that the conditions are numerous and uncharacteristic of the real world. In reality, different economies can be expected to have different relative prices in the absence of internal controls, and an equality of relative prices fails to indicate that macroeconomic controls have left the home price of exports unaltered. Consequently, a general test of the merit of the home price as a standard of fair value remains to be discovered. Until one emerges, the Treasury Department can only utilize the home price when it can observe that a particular industry is free from government influences or when it can assess the impact of controls from their nature.

At present, then, the Treasury Department may be in error in failing to consider the home-market price of imports from Eastern-bloc countries which contain essentially free-market economies with specific controls placed on particular industries. In this instance, as Anthony suggests, it may be possible to assess whether, and to what extent, internal policies affect the home price as a standard of fair value. The price may be rejected in the case of state monopolies, accepted when the control is a price floor, and amended in the instance of subsidization. But when the economy is subject to ubiquitous planning—so that the volume of interindustry transfers is predetermined and goods and factor prices are just shadow prices—Anthony's criticism of current policy is unjustified. In this case, the unassessable effects of indirect controls make costs and prices meaningless, regardless of any direct controls that can be accounted for.

Similarly, when controlled economies contain firms that are essentially autonomous producers and sellers, export prices to third-party nations may serve as standards of fair value. But contrary to Feller's assertion, fair value cannot be based on such export prices from planned economies in which this autonomy is lacking. With respect to East-West trade, it may be reasonable to assume that planned economies generally sell at the highest obtainable price in order to maximize earnings. But unlike the case of exports from Western firms, it cannot be concluded from this that the export price is a nondumping price, however long the period for which it has prevailed. For exporters in command economies are under no obligation to cover costs or earn a normal return. Even if they were obliged to do so, there is no guarantee that their costs are rationally determined by productivity and factor abundance.[b] Consequently, the presumption cannot be established that the export prices of such economies, even export prices of long standing, are fair value prices from the point of view of the free-market mechanism.

The Treasury Department, then, should consider home and third-country export prices as a basis for the fair value of American imports when the imports come from Eastern-bloc nations with substantially free markets. On the other hand, its rejection of these prices when reviewing imports from extensively planned economies is warranted, but the substitute measure of fair value that it employes is not ideal. For the price charged by firms in a free-market economy similar to the command economy may not reflect the costs and profits that would obtain in the planned economy were they rationally determined. And, moreover, even when prices in a comparable free-market economy do reflect such costs and profits, it cannot be said that the command economy is not dumping if it exports at the free-market economy's price, for the command economy may yet be charging less on exports to the United States than it could have obtained elsewhere.

Overall, the Treasury Department errs to some extent—although by no means gravely—in calculating the average revenue obtained by exporters in markets outside of the United States. In addition, in a number of respects, it incorrectly adjusts this value to provide a standard by which to measure profit-sacrificing behavior in American markets.

---

[b] Feller acknowledges both of these points early in his article (pp. 118–22), although he ignores them in concluding that Eastern-bloc export prices to third parties are a useful measure of fair value.

In addition, recent writings on Soviet dumping and trade policy indicate that export prices bear no relationship to costs, however determined; thus, they cannot be taken as a measure of fair value, Feller's reasoning aside. In this regard, see Andrea Boltho, *Foreign Trade Criteria in Socialist Countries* (Cambridge, England: Cambridge University Press, 1971), chaps. 3–4; and J. Wilczynski, "Dumping and Central Planning," *Journal of Political Economy* 74 (June 1966):250–65.

Theoretically, the price normally charged elsewhere may be an inadequate standard by which to judge profit-sacrificing behavior on American sales for two and only two reasons. First, the FOB factory cost of selling merchandise for export to the United States may differ from the cost pertaining to other sales. Second, the merchandise sold in export to the United States may be more or less valuable to all potential purchasers than the merchandise used to compute its fair value. Consequently, the basic measure of fair value should be adjusted to compensate for these differences when they exist, but should remain unaltered otherwise.

In light of this principle, the manner in which the Treasury Department adjusts its estimate of fair value to account for quantity discounts granted on large-lot sales to the United States is at once too generous and too restrictive. It should be recalled that the Treasury's initial estimate of an import's fair value is the price charged on home-market sales made in "the usual wholesale quantities." To the extent that selling in the United States in larger quantities lowers the exporter's unit cost, he clearly does not cut his profit margin by reducing his price below the home level. Consequently, the Treasury is correct in reducing its fair-value estimate by the full amount of any discounts that are cost-justified.

Quantity discounts unaccompanied by cost savings, however, decrease the average profit earned on sales to the United States, and they should not be allowed for, as such, in calculating fair value. Rather, the exporting producer may make a certain percentage of his non-United States sales in quantities other than the usual wholesale amounts. He may give quantity discounts on these sales that are not cost-justified. And to this extent, basing fair value exclusively on transactions involving the usual wholesale quantities will overestimate the average price received by the exporting concern. Thus, in this respect, quantity discounts that are not premised on cost savings should be accounted for. The correct procedure is to include the price on sales made in abnormally large quantities abroad in the Treasury Department's initial estimate of foreign prices in proportion to the ratio of such sales to the firm's overall business. At present, however, the Treasury allows for the full value of quantity discounts, without requiring cost justification, if similar discounts have been granted on 20% of home-market sales during the six months proceding the dumping complaint. Conversely, it refuses to allow for such discounts if this condition is not met. Consequently, current procedures for adjusting for quantity discounts will lead to an underestimation of the fair value of imports in some cases and to an overestimation in others.

In adjusting for differences in other circumstances of sale, correct procedure is to alter the initial estimate of fair value only by the amount that such differences increase or decrease the cost of exporting to the United States or the value of the merchandise and ancillary services sold to

American purchasers. As in the case of quantity discounts, there is no reason within the logic of using dumping as a signal of profit-sacrificing behavior for adjusting for circumstances of sale that have neither effect or for failing to adjust when differences in circumstances of sale have these effects, regardless of how the effect might occur. Thus, present policy, which limits adjustments for differences in circumstances of sale to those bearing a "direct" relationship to the sales involved, is unjustified. As has been observed, under this policy, differences in bad-debt ratios on home and foreign sales would probably not be allowed for, although the cost savings due to such differences may be quantifiable.

Finally, while the Antidumping Act does not require the Secretary of the Treasury to use foreign-market values in discovering dumping, it does stipulate that any antidumping duties must be equal to the difference between an import's foreign-market value and its American selling price.[36] The effect of this provision is to force exporters to sell in the United States at prices equal to those charged elsewhere, and this in turn erases the threat of profit sacrificing in the average sense. The logic of regulating dumping, however, does not indicate that foreign concerns should be prevented from earning less than their normal rate of profit when selling in the United States. Rather, the existence of dumping merely suggests that the imports in question may be detrimental to welfare and their impact on the domestic economy merits inspection. If it proves to be the case that the imports are, in fact, injurious, further harm should be prevented, hopefully with a minimum price increase to the American consumer whose welfare the Act is ultimately supposed to protect. Thus, the magnitude of antidumping duties should be that amount which is just sufficient to alleviate the injury that the dumping causes, but not necessarily the dumping. The difference between a good's import price and its foreign-market value is properly the maximum penalty that should be exacted, but the imposition of a lesser levy should be permitted if adequate to remedy the import's detrimental effect.

### Endnotes

1. This aspect of the Act was changed only once, by an amendment contained in the *Trade Act of 1974, Statutes at Large* 88, sec. 321, 2043 (1974).
2. Ibid., sec. 321 (b).
3. Ibid.
4. Ibid., sec. 321 (c).
5. *Antidumping Act, U.S. Code,* vol. 19, sec. 161 (1970).
6. Ibid., sec. 160.

7. James Pomeroy Hendrick, "The United States Antidumping Act," *American Journal of International Law* 58 (1964):920, n. 20.

8. *Customs Simplification Act, Title III, Amendments to the Antidumping Act, 1921, Statutes at Large* 68, sec. 201 (a), 1138 (1954).

9. See the regulations of the Treasury Department defining fair value that were adopted on April 8, 1955. *Antidumping Regulations, Code of Federal Regulations,* Title 19, sec. 14.7 (1955); see also Hendrick, n. 20; and U.S., Congress, Senate, Committee on Finance, *Antidumping Act-Amendment,* S. Rept. 1619 to Accompany H.R. 6006, 85th Cong., 2d sess., 1958, pp. 1–3.

10. U.S., Congress, House, *A Bill to Amend Certain Provisions of the Antidumping Act, 1921, to Provide for Greater Certainty, Speed, and Efficiency in the Enforcement Thereof, and for Other Purposes,* H.R. 6006, 85th Cong., 1st sess., 1957, pp. 1–11; see also, U.S., Congress, Senate, Committee on Finance, *Antidumping Act-Amendment;* and Hendrick, p. 920, nn. 19, 20.

11. These changes are described and discussed in the following sources: Hendrick, pp. 922–23; James C. Connor and Gerald Buschlinger, "The United States Antidumping Act: A Timely Survey," *Virginia Journal of International Law* 7 (December 1966):125; U.S., Department of the Treasury, "Antidumping Duties," in *International Economic Policy in an Interdependent World,* comp. U.S., Commission on International Trade and Investment Policy, 2 vols. (Washington, D.C.: Government Printing Office, 1971), 1:407–408; Bart S. Fisher, "The Antidumping Law of the United States: A Legal and Economic Analysis," *Law and Policy in International Business* 5 (1973):98–99; and *Antidumping Regulations, Code of Federal Regulations,* Title 19, secs. 153.7 (b), 153.8 (1973).

12. *Antidumping Act, U.S. Code Annotated,* vol. 19, sec. 164 (1970).

13. Ibid., sec. 165.

14. Ibid., sec. 164.

15. Fisher, pp. 95–96, n. 47.

16. See Ronald L. Styne, "The Antidumping Act: Problems of Administration and Proposals for Change," *Stanford Law Review* 17 (April 1965); R. A. Anthony, "The American Response to Dumping from Capitalist and Socialist Countries; Substantive Premises and Restructured Procedures after the 1967 GATT Code," *Cornell Law Review* 54 (January 1969):200–201, n. 169; and *Antidumping Regulations, Code of Federal Regulations,* Title 19, sec. 153.5 (b) (1975).

17. *Trade Act of 1974,* sec. 321 (d).

18. *Antidumping Regulations, Code of Federal Regulations,* Title 19, secs. 153.3 (b), 153.4 (b), and 153.9 (1975).

19. Ibid., sec. 153.7.

20. Ibid., sec. 153.8.

21. Fisher, p. 99.

22. Jacob Viner, *Dumping: A Problem in International Trade* (Chicago: University of Chicago Press, 1923), p. 264.

23. *Kleberg* v. *United States,* 21 C.C.P.A. (customs) 110, 114, 71 F. 2d 332, 335 (1933).

24. See Peter D. Ehrenhaft, "Protection Against International Price Discrimination: United States Countervailing and Antidumping Duties," *Columbia Law Review* 58 (1958):63–67; and James A. Kohn, "The Antidumping Act: Its Administration and Place in American Trade Policy," *Michigan Law Review* 60 (February 1962):414–17.

25. Ehrenhaft, p. 66; and Kohn, p. 416.

26. Ehrenhaft, p. 66.

27. Kohn, pp. 411, 416–17, 437.

28. U.S., Congress, House, *A Bill Imposing Temporary Duties on Certain Agricultural Products to Meet Present Emergencies, and to Provide Revenue; to Regulate Commerce with Foreign Countries; to Prevent Dumping of Foreign Merchandise on the Markets of the United States; and for Other Purposes,* H.R. 2435, 67th Cong., 1st sess., 1921, Title II, secs. 207, 208.

29. U.S., Congress, Senate, *Emergency Tariff Bill,* S. Rept. 16 to Accompany H.R. 2435, 67th Cong., 1st sess., 1921, p. 10.

30. U.S., Congress, Senate, Committee on Finance, *Emergency Tariff and Antidumping, Hearings Before a Subcommittee on the Senate Committee on Finance on H.R. 2435,* 67th Cong., 1st sess., 1921, pp. 9–14.

31. See Styne, pp. 733–34; Anthony, pp. 159–231 passim; and Peter B. Feller, "The Antidumping Act and the Future of East-West Trade," *Michigan Law Review* 66 (November 1967):114–40.

32. Anthony, pp. 198–207.

33. Feller, pp. 126–29.

34. Ibid., pp. 129–33.

35. Anthony, pp. 205–10.

36. *Antidumping Act, U.S. Code Annotated,* vol. 19, sec. 161 (a) (1970).

# 5 Recommendations for Improving United States Antidumping Policy

Having analyzed the definition of dumping contained in the Antidumping Act, it is time to offer suggestions for improving the efficacy of this instrument of commercial policy. In this chapter, potentially beneficial revisions in the Act are set forth. The conclusions reached previously are used to explain their rationale, and attention is devoted to the merit of the GATT Antidumping Code as a guide to reform.

## Definition of Dumping Employed in American Proceedings

In Chapter 3, it was concluded that dumped imports are more likely to lower welfare in the importing nation than are single-priced imports because dumping permits profit-sacrificing export pricing. Accordingly, the existence of dumping can rightfully be employed by an importing nation as a signal that the effect of the imports on domestic welfare merits inspection. When used in this manner, the term "dumping" should be defined as the pricing of exports to the country in question below the average price received in other markets customarily supplied by the exporting concern on the sale of merchandise of similar use-value and factory cost.

The United States Antidumping Act, however, merely directs the Secretary of the Treasury to determine whether the American selling price of imports is less than their "fair value." Since the Act does not define "fair value," the construction of this term is left to the Secretary.

In investigating dumping, the Secretary of the Treasury has continually interpreted the fair value of imports to be synonymous with their foreign-market value, a term that the Act describes with some precision and which it specifies is to be used in calculating the pertinent amount of antidumping duties. In general, foreign-market value, as described in the Act, is an acceptable measure of the average revenue which the exporter earns in the non-United States markets that he regularly supplies, and, thus, the Treasury Department's interpretation of fair value has been commendable. Nevertheless, in a number of respects, the definition of foreign-market value that has emerged from the Act and Treasury Department regulations is not ideal.

In this regard, the most serious error made in defining foreign-market value has been to assign too much importance to the home-market price of imports. In fact, at present, both the Antidumping Act and the GATT Code err in this manner, for both documents state that an import's foreign value should be based exclusively on its home price whenever this price can be reasonably determined.[1] Moreover, in applying the Act, the Treasury Department does not ameliorate the impact of this provision, for it customarily bases foreign-market values on home-market prices whenever home sales are 5% or more of all non-United States sales.

When a firm customarily sells its output at home and in a number of export markets other than the United States, the price that it expects to receive per unit of output, and upon which it bases its profitability and continued survival, will depend on the prices garnered in third-party nations no less than on its home-market price. Thus, there is no reason to single out the home-market price as the singular standard by which to measure dumping. In fact, since foreign demand is often more elastic than home demand, to do so may lead to an affirmation of dumping when profit-sacrificing behavior is absent, and there is no reason to view the United States imports askance. Consequently, the Antidumping Act should be revised to direct the Secretary of the Treasury to base the foreign-market value of imports on a weighted average of the prices obtaining in markets in which the exporter normally makes a significant portion of his non-United States sales. In this aspect of the antidumping process, American procedures should be altered in a manner that conflicts with the recommendation of the GATT Code.

Furthermore, when an import's foreign-market value cannot be derived from its home price or the prices charged in non-United States markets, the Act stipulates that its "constructed value" is to be used in lieu thereof. The Act defines the constructed value of an import as the sum of its cost of production and packaging for shipment to the United States, general expenses of not less than 10% of direct costs, and profits of not less that 8% of total cost. The definition contained in the GATT Code is similar to that of the Act, except that it specifies that constructed value should only include the customary level of general expenses and profits in the district of manufacture.[2]

Unlike the Act, then the GATT Code does not place a lower limit on the magnitude of general expenses and profits to be included in a good's constructed value: and this is an important difference between the two documents. The Act's proviso may be necessary to prevent the underestimation of general expenses and profits for the purpose of avoiding antidumping duties. But when the cost and profit data submitted by the exporter are reliable and indicate a lesser rate of profit and general expenses, this provision will lead to an estimate of foreign-market value that exceeds the average return customarily obtained by the exporting concern. Accordingly, the Act should be amended along the lines taken by the GATT Code. In this respect, a safeguard against the problem anticipated by the Act can be retained, and its present equivocation eliminated, if it is altered to stipulate that constructed value should include the customary level of general expenses and profits in the district of manufacture, except when there is reason to suspect that the exporter has misrepresented these figures; in which case the firm's general expenses and profits will be estimated as 10% of direct costs and 8% of all costs, respectively.

In the case of imports from command economies, the Treasury Department has felt that neither the home price of the goods nor their non-United States export price can be used to estimate their foreign-market value, since neither price is freely determined by the forces of supply and demand. In additon, the irrationality of resource prices in command economies and impediments to acquiring cost data have prevented the Treasury from calculating the constructed value of their exports. Consequently, in inquiring into the existence of dumping, the Secretary of the Treasury has customarily based the foreign-market value of imports from Eastern-bloc nations on prices charged by similar free-market economies on domestic and foreign sales of like merchandise. And in 1974, Congress amended the Antidumping Act to define the foreign-market value of imports from command economies in accordance with the Treasury's estimating procedures.[a]

In general, the Treasury Department's refusal to base foreign-market value on command-economy prices is well taken. Nevertheless, such prices should not be summarily rejected as a measure of foreign-market value; for in some instances, the home and export prices of goods produced in essentially planned economies may not be affected by government controls, however widespread. Moreover, even when these prices are affected by government controls, prices charged by a similar free-market economy will not necessarily reflect production costs in the command economy under review or the revenue that can be earned by selling in free-world markets. Consequently, the Antidumping Act should be altered to direct the Secretary of the Treasury to base foreign-market value on the home and export price of merchandise produced in command economies whenever it can be shown that existing controls do not affect these prices; and, otherwise, to rely on an average of prices in the free-world markets in which the imports could be alternatively sold.

In addition, in amending its basic estimates of foreign-market value, the Treasury Department currently refuses to allow for differences in circumstances of sale when such differences are indirectly related to the

---

[a] The GATT Code does not contain any provisions concerning the measurement of dumping on imports from planned economies.

sales involved. It refuses to make allowance for quantity discounts that are not cost-justified if they are granted on less than 20% of non-United States sales in the six months preceding its investigation. And it grants full allowance for such discounts if they meet this criterion, in spite of the fact that such discounts do not reduce the average non-United States price on a one-to-one basis. None of these policies is particularly conducive to constructing an estimate of the average price earned by foreign concerns on the sale of merchandise.

Present errors in the adjustment of the base price to arrive at a final estimate of foreign-market value would be eliminated, however, if the Secretary of the Treasury followed the directive of the GATT Code that every difference in circumstances of sale affecting price comparability should be considered on its merits.[3] In effect, the adoption of this policy would mean that the basic estimate of foreign-market value would only be adjusted if the Secretary had to reason to believe that (1) United States imports cannot be sold in other markets at the same price as are the goods sold therein, or (2) FOB factory costs differ between goods sold to the United States and elsewhere. In terms of present Treasury Department practice, this would necessitate the elimination of the provision that only differences in circumstances of sale that are directly related to the transactions in question will be considered in adjusting the foreign-market-value estimate. With respect to quantity discounts, it would mean that strict cost justificaiton would be required for a reduction in the estimate of foreign-market value on a dollar-for-dollar basis with the discounts claimed on exports to the United States. Otherwise, the granting of discounts on large-lot sales would only affect an import's foreign-market value by lowering the average price received at home or on export sales to third-party nations.

Finally, at present, the Antidumping Act requires that any additional duties must be equal to the margin of dumping found by the Treasury Department. Such duties, however, should only be assessed in an amount sufficient to alleviate the injury that led to their imposition, since the purpose of antidumping proceedings is not to penalize dumping, but to preclude an injury therefrom. This is, in fact, the position taken by the GATT Code,[4] and thus the Act's provision on the magnitude of antidumping duties should be revised to conform to the Code's dictates.

## Injury Requirement of the Antidumping Act

The American definition of dumping is susceptible to improvement along the lines suggested above. Nevertheless, this facet of the antidumping process has been the subject of numerous, constructive revisions in recent years, and as a result, it is not in need of extensive reform. The same cannot be said of the injury requirement contained in the Antidumping Act, for it was ill conceived at the Act's inception and has not been altered since.

In our theoretical analysis, it was established that dumping presents an extraordinary threat to welfare in the importing nation for two reasons. It increases the chance that the exporting concern will monopolize the import market, and it increases the probability that the supply of imports will be temporary and will disrupt domestic production.

At the same time, it was observed that dumping does not generally differ from normal importation; that is, usually dumped imports will not cause monopolization or market destabilization but will raise welfare in the importing country. Moreover, dumping that benefits society may well harm domestic producers by reducing their prices and sales. Thus, there is no necessary correspondence between an injury to native firms and an injury to social welfare. Consequently, antidumping legislation should not prohibit dumping, nor should it prohibit dumping simply because it harms domestic concerns. Rather, such legislation should stipulate that dumping should only be penalized when one of the deleterious effects associated with the practice occurs or is in the offing.

The United States Antidumping Act, however, only directs the International Trade Commission to investigate whether "an industry in the United States is being or is likely to be injured, or is prevented from being established" by dumping. Noticeably, this provision focuses on an injury to American producers, rather than on an injury to the domestic market or domestic production patterns; and it fails to specify the nature of the injury that merits antidumping duties. Accordingly, in addressing the injury issue, the ITC is given leeway to make a positive finding when dumping does no more than injure domestic concerns, and, in fact, the ITC's record over the last twenty years suggests that it has frequently done so.[5] Consequently, the focus of the Act's injury provision is misleading. The wording of the injury requirement is too general to ensure the optimal regulation of dumping; it is in dire need of reform.

As to the appropriate revisions in this aspect of the Act, it is instructive to note that there are four major differences between the provisions of the Act and those of the GATT Antidumping Code.

First, article VI, paragraph 6 of the GATT requires that dumping must create a "material injury" for additional duties to be applied, while the United States law only states that there should be an "injury."[6]

Second, in contrast to the Act, which makes no reference to how an injury is to be assessed, article 3(b) of the Code stipulates that an evaluation of the effect of dumping "shall be based on ... all factors having a bearing on the state of the industry in question." In addition, the Code lists a large number of criteria as pertinent to judging the injury issue.[7]

Third, article 12 of the Code permits nations that export at fair value to apply to an importing nation for antidumping protection if they are being injured by less-than-fair-value imports from other countries. It provides that the decision as to whether to proceed with an investigation shall rest with the importing country and, if an inquiry is made, the effect of the dumping on the entire industry in the third-party nation must be considered.[8] In contrast, the United States Act makes no provision for extending antidumping protection to exporters who sell in the United States at fair value.

Fourth, the Code specifies that the domestic industry which is examined for the effects of foreign dumping should include "all producers of like products" or "those . . . whose collective output of like products constitutes a major portion of the total domestic production of those products." The Code provides for two exceptions to this rule: (1) that the industry may be interpreted so as to exclude producers who are importers of the dumped goods, and (2) that it may be divided into competitive market areas, regarded as separate industries, when producers in these market areas sell all or almost all of their output therein, while producers located elsewhere sell none or almost none of their output therein.[9] On the other hand, the Antidumping Act does not elaborate on the meaning of "an industry in the United States," and, as a result, the ITC may unreasonably limit the industry under review, thus magnifying the chance of a finding of injury.

Given these differences between the Act and the Code, it appears that a harmonization of the American injury requirement with that contained in the Code will improve United States antidumping policy to some degree. Extending the coverage of the Act to foreign concerns that sell in the United States will increase America's protection against monopolization. Requiring the ITC to appraise the overall health of the domestic industry will safeguard against findings of injury based on adverse effects of dumping that do not threaten society's welfare. Requiring ITC to select the industry relevant to its inquiry in accordance with the Code's directives will furnish additional protection against unwarranted affirmation of injury.

Nevertheless, although greater conformity to the GATT Antidumping Code will improve the Antidumping Act in these ways, it will not provide a broad enough reform to preclude an inappropriate use of the statute. For, basically, the Act permits a protectionist application because it fails to specify that "injury" means an anticompetitive effect in the import market, or, alternatively, a temporary market disruption without the provision of a long-run supply of imports. With respect to the meaning of injury, however, the Code merely provides that a "material injury" should be considered necessary for the imposition of antidumping duties. Thus, the Code only defines the appropraite degree of injury, and does not comment on the type of injury that should obtain for a positive finding to be warranted. Moreover, the remainder of the Code's provisions concern specific practices to be employed in addressing the injury issue, not the type of injury that should be prevented.

While conformity to the GATT Antidumping Code is a laudable goal, a reform of the United States injury requirement should surpass a mere harmonization of American proceedings with the international standard. The United States Antidumping Act should be rewritten to state that the ITC shall investigate whether dumping injures or is likely to injure a market in the United States, and not a domestic industry. It should also specify that an injury consists of either (1) a temporary market disturbance due to the dumping of imports that will not be permanently supplied, or (2) a change in the structure of the market that reduces or threatens to reduce competition.

Referring to the first type of injury, the Act should state that the injury may be evaluated by appraising price and sales trends in the relevant market alone and that the prices and sales of both domestic producers and exporters who sell at fair value should be considered. Regarding the second type of injury, the Act should specify that the effect of dumping on competition should be assessed by reviewing the growth in, and level of, the dumper's relative market share and trends in profits, employment, capacity utilization, turnovers, customer contact, and unit cost respecting all firms that sell in competition with the dumper. Furthermore, the law should state that price and sales trends should only be utilized to assess dumping's effect on competition if sufficient data on the above variables cannot be obtained. And it should provide that the ITC should only find "injury" if the dumper's present or prospective market share indicates that he may be able to control the market price, or if the prosperity of rival sellers is or is likely to be lessened to a degree sufficient to impair their ability to engage in effective competition.

These are the essential changes that must be made in the antidumping policy of the United States. Even with such changes, American antidumping policy will continue to differ from the provisions of the GATT Code in some important respects. Nevertheless, it will be free from the danger of a protectionist application, and it will be an effective instrument for maximizing welfare in a nation that supports trade liberalization through the reduction of nontariff barriers to importation. In the absence of such changes, the administration of the Antidumping Act may reflect, in part, the singular concern for the health of domestic industry that led to its enactment over half a century ago.

118

**Endnotes**

1. Contracting Parties to the General Agreement on Tariffs and Trade, *Agreement on the Implementation of Article VI* (Antidumping Code) (Geneva: General Agreement on Tariffs and Trade, 1969), art. 2 (a), (d) (hereafter cited as GATT, *Antidumping Code*).

2. Ibid., art. 2 (d).

3. Ibid., art. 2 (f).

4. Ibid., art. 8 (a).

5. For a detailed discussion of the injury determinations made by the ITC between 1955 and 1974 see William A. Wares, "An Evaluation of the Provisions and Recent Administrative History of the United States Antidumping Act of 1921" (Ph.D. diss., University of Michigan, 1976).

6. See Contracting Parties to the General Agreement on Tariffs and Trade, *Analytical Index to the General Agreement (Third Revision)* (Geneva: Contracting Parties to the General Agreement on Tariffs and Trade, 1970), p. 36.

7. GATT, *Antidumping Code,* art. 3 (b).

8. Ibid., art. 12.

9 Ibid., art. 4.

# Bibliography

# Bibliography

**Articles**

Anthony, R. A. "The American Response to Dumping from Capitalist and Social Countries; Substantive Premises and Restructured Procedures after the 1967 GATT Code." *Cornell Law Review* 54 (January 1969):159–231.

Clemens, Eli W. "Price Discrimination and the Multiproduct Firm." *Review of Economic Studies* 19 (1950–51):1–11.

Cocks, R. A., and Johnson, Harry G. "A Note on Dumping and Social Welfare." *Canadian Journal of Economics* 1 (February 1972):137–40.

"Comment—The Antidumping Act: Tariff or Antitrust Law?" *Yale Law Journal* 74 (1965):707–24.

Connor, James C., and Buschlinger, Gerald. "The United States Antidumping Act: A Timely Survey." *Virginia Journal of International Law* 7 (December 1965):117–38.

Copithorne, L. W. "International Corporate Transfer Prices and Government Policy." *Canadian Journal of Economics* 4 (August 1971):324–41.

de Jonge, H. W. "The Significance of Dumping in International Trade." *Journal of World Trade Law* 2 (1968):161–88.

de Scitovsky, Tibor. "A Reconsideration of the Theory of Tariffs." *Review of Economic Studies* 9 (Summer 1942):89–110.

Edwards, E. O. "The Analysis of Output under Discrimination." *Econometrica* 18 (1950):163–72.

Ehrenhaft, Peter D. "Protection Against International Price Discrimination; United States Countervailing and Antidumping Duties." *Columbia Law Review* 58 (1958):44–76.

Enke, Steven. "Monopolistic Output and International Trade." *Quarterly Journal of Economics* 60 (February 1946):233–49.

Feller, Peter B. "The Antidumping Act and the Future of East-West Trade." *Michigan Law Review* 66 (November 1967):114–40.

Fisher, Bart S. "The Antidumping Law of the United States: A Legal and Economic Analysis." *Law and Policy in International Business* 5 (1973):85–154.

Hendrick, James Pomeroy. "The United States Antidumping Act." *American Journal of International Law* 58 (1964):914–34.

Keyes, Lucile Sheppard. "Price Discrimination in Law and Economics." *Southern Economic Journal* 27 (April 1961):320–28.

Kohn, James A. "The Antidumping Act: Its Administration and Place in a American Trade Policy." *Michigan Law Review* 60 (February 1962):207–38.

Leontief, W. W. "The Theory of Limited and Unlimited Discrimination." *Quarterly Journal of Economics* 54 (May 1940):490–501.

Maroni, Y. R. "Discrimination under Market Interdependence." *Quarterly Journal of Economics* 62 (November 1947):95–117.

Rose, Sanford. "The Rewarding Strategies of Multinationalism." *Fortune* 78 (September 1968):100–106.

Sandmo, Agnar. "On the Theory of the Competitive Firm under Price Uncertainty." *American Economic Review* 61 (March 1971):65–73.

Simkin, C. G. F. "Some Aspects and Generalizations of the Theory of Discrimination." *Review of Economic Studies* 15 (1947–48):1–13.

Stolper, Wolfgang F., and Samuelson, Paul A. "Protection and Real Wages." *Review of Economic Studies* 9 (November 1941):58–71.

Styne, Ronald L. "The Antidumping Act: Problems of Administration and Proposals for Change." *Stanford Law Review* 17 (April 1965): 1965):730–49.

"Trusts and Protection." *Protectionist* 16 (November 1904):361–62.

Walters, A. A. "Production and Cost Functions." *Econometrica* 31 (January 1963):1–66.

Weeks, James Keith. "Introduction to the Antidumping Law: A Form of Protection for the American Manufacturer." *Albany Law Review* 35 (1970–71):182–92.

Wilczynski, J. "Dumping and Central Planning." *Journal of Political Economy* 74 (June 1966):250–65.

Yntema, Y. O. "The Influence of Dumping on Monopoly Price." *Journal of Political Economy* 36 (December 1928):686–98.

## Books

⟿Austin, O. P. *Economics of World Trade*. New York: Business Training Corp., 1916.

Bidwell, Percy Wells. *What the Tariff Means to American Industries*. New York: Harper and Co., 1956.

Boltho, Andrea. *Foreign Trade Criteria in Socialist Countries*. Cambridge, England: Cambridge University Press, 1971.

Chamberlin, Edward. *The Theory of Monopolistic Competition*. 8th ed. Cambridge: Harvard University Press, 1962.

Culbertson, William Smith. *Commercial Policy in Wartime and After*. New York: D. Appleton and Co., 1919.

Curtiss, W. M. *The Tariff Idea*. New York: The Foundation for Economic Education, Inc., 1953.

Dawson, William Harbutt. *The Evolution of Modern Germany* New York: S C. Schribner's Sons, 1914.

Flugel, Felix, and Faulkner, Harold U., eds. *Readings in the Economic and Social History of the United States*. New York: Harper Bros. Publishers, 1929.

Haberler, Gottfried von. *The Theory of International Trade*. London: William Hodge and Co., Ltd., 1936.

Heaton, Herbert. *Economic History of Europe*. rev. ed. New York: Harper and Row, Publishers, 1948.

Jackson, John H. *World Trade and the Law of GATT*. New York: Bobbs-Merrill Co., 1969.

Kemp, Murray C. *The Pure Theory of International Trade*. Englewood Cliffs, N.J.: Prentice-Hall, Inc., 1964.

Kindleberger, Charles P. *International Economics*. 3d ed. Homewood, Ill.: Richard D. Irwin, Inc., 1963.

Larkin, John Day. *The President's Control of the Tariff*. Cambridge: Harvard University Press, 1936.

Miles, Roger Q. "Tariff Issues Plainly Stated." In *Readings in the Economic and Social History of the United States*, p. 536. Edited by Felix Flugel and Harold U. Faulkner. New York: Harper Bros. Publishers, 1929.

Robinson, Joan. *The Economics of Imperfect Competition*. London: Macmillan and Co., Ltd., 1933.

Scherer, Frederick M. *Industrial Market Structure and Economic Performance*. Chicago: Rand McNally and Co., 1970.

Scoville, John, and Sargent, Noel. *Facts and Fancy in the TNEC Monographs*. New York: National Association of Manufacturers, 1942.

Seavy, William Arthur. *Dumping since the War; The GATT and National Laws*. Oakland: Office Services Corp., 1970.

Stocking, George W., and Watkins, Myron W. *Cartels or Competition?* New York: Twentieth Century Fund, 1948.

Taussig, F. W. *Some Aspects of the Tariff Question*. 3d ed. Cambridge: Harvard University Press, 1931.

Viner, Jacob. *Dumping: A Problem in International Trade*. Chicago: University of Chicago Press, 1923.

Wares, William A. "An Evaluation of the Provisions and Recent Administrative History of the United States Antidumping Act of 1921." Ph.D. dissertation, University of Michigan, 1976.

### GATT Publications

Contracting Parties to the General Agreement on Tariffs and Trade. *Agreement on the Implementation of Article VI (Antidumping Code).* Geneva: General Agreement on Tariffs and Trade, 1969.

_____. *Analytical Index to the General Agreement (Third Revision).* Geneva: Contracting Parties to the General Agreement on Tariffs and Trade, 1970.

_____. *Antidumping and Countervailing Duties.* Geneva: Contracting Parties to the General Agreement on Tariffs and Trade, 1958.


### Judicial Decisions

*Kleberg* v. *United States.* 21 C.C.P.A. (Customs) 110–16; 71 F 2d 332–35 (1933).


### United States Government Documents and Publications

*Antidumping Act. U.S. Code,* vol. 19 (1970).

*Antidumping Act. U.S. Code, Annotated,* vol. 19 (1970).

*Antidumping Regulations. Code of Federal Regulations,* Title 19 (1955).

*Antidumping Regulations. Code of Federal Regulations,* Title 19 (1973).

*Antidumping Regulations. Code of Federal Regulations,* Title 19 (1975)

*Customs Simplification Act, Title III, Amendments to the Antidumping Act, 1921. Statutes at Large,* vol. 68 (1954).

Gilbert, Milton. "A Sample Study of Differences Between Domestic and Export Pricing Policies of United States Corporations." In *Investigations of Concentration of Economic Power,* monograph no. 6, pp. 3–93. Compiled by U.S., Congress, Senate, Temporary National Economic Committee. Washington, D.C.: Government Printing Office, 1941.

Holzman, F.D. "Some Financial Aspects of Soviet Foreign Trade." In *Comparisons of United States and Soviet Economies,* pt. 2, pp. 427–66. Compiled by U.S., Congress, Joint Economic Committee. Washington, D.C.: Government Printing Office, 1959.

*Trade Act of 1974. Statutes at Large,* vol. 88 (1974).

U.S., Congress. House. *A Bill Imposing Temporary Duties on Certain Agricultural Products to Meet Present Emergencies, and to Provide*

*Revenue; to Regulate Commerce with Foreign Countries; to Prevent Dumping of Foreign Merchandise on the Markets of the United States; to Regulate the Value of Foreign Money; and for Other Purposes.* H.R. 2435, 67th Cong., 1st sess., 1921.

_____. *A Bill to Amend Certain Provisions of the Antidumping Act, 1921, to Provide for Greater Certainty, Speed, and Efficiency in the Enforcement Thereof, and for Other Purposes.* H.R. 6006, 85th Cong., 1st sess., 1957.

_____. *A Bill to Provide Revenue and Encourage Domestic Industries by the Elimination, through the Assessment of Special Duties, of Unfair Competition and for Other Purposes.* H.R. 10918, 66th Cong., 2d sess., 1919.

_____. Committee on Ways and Means. *Antidumping and Undervaluation Hearings. Hearings Before a Subcommittee of the House Committee on Ways and Means.* 66th Cong., 1st sess., 1919.

_____. Committee on Ways and Means. *Tariff Hearings, Undervaluation and Antidumping Duties. Hearings Before a Subcommittee of the House Committee on Ways and Means.* 62d Cong., 3d sess., 1913, pt. VI.

_____. Debate on a proposed amendment to the Antidumping Act. H.R. 6006, 85th Cong., 1st sess., 29 August 1957. *Congressional Record,* vol. 103.

_____. *Emergency Tariff Bill,* H. Rept. 1 to Accompany H.R. 2435, 67th Cong., 1st sess., 1921.

_____. Mr. Collier speaking on the proposed antidumping amendments of 1964. 88th Cong., 2d sess., 14 April 1964. *Congressional Record,* vol. 110.

_____. Mr. Fordney introducing the antidumping bill proposed in 1919, and the subsequent debate thereon. H.R. 10918, 66th Cong., 2d sess., 9 December 1919. *Congressional Record,* vol. 59.

_____. Mr. Harter speaking in favor of his antidumping bill. H.R. 8603, 74th Cong., 2d sess., 22 August 1935. *Congressional Record,* vol. 79.

U.S. Congress. Senate. *Antidumping Act—Amendment,* S. Rept. 1619 to Accompany H.R. 6006, 85th Cong., 2d sess., 1956.

_____. *Antidumping Legislation and Other Import Regulations in the United States and Foreign Countries.* S. Doc. 112, 73d Cong., 2d sess., 1934.

_____. Committee on Finance. *Emergency Tariff and Antidumping. Hearings Before a Subcommittee of the Senate Committee on Finance on H.R. 2435.* 67th Cong., 1st sess., 1921.

126

_____. Committee on Finance. *Tariff Act of 1921, Dye Embargo. Hearings Before a Subcommittee of the Senate Committee on Finance on H.R. 7546.* 67th Cong., 1st sess., 1921.

_____. Debate on the proposed antidumping act. Title II of H.R. 2435, 67th Cong., 1st sess., 4–7 May 1921. *Congressional Record,* vol. 61.

_____. Debate on the proposed antidumping act. Title II of H.R. 2435, 67th Cong., 1st sess., 9–11 May 1921. *Congressional Record,* vol. 61.

_____. *Duties on Imports,* S. Rept. 510 to Accompany H.R. 10918, 66th Cong., 2d sess., 1919.

_____. *Emergency Tariff Bill,* S. Rept. 16 to Accompany H.R. 2435, 67th Cong., 1st sess., 1921.

_____. Senator Knox speaking in favor of the embargo on dyestuffs. 67th Cong., 1st sess., 9 May 1921. *Congressional Record,* vol. 61.

_____. Senator Scott speaking on a bill to amend the Antidumping Act. S. 2045, 89th Cong., 1st sess., 26 May 1965. *Congressional Record,* vol. 111.

_____. Senator Smoot speaking on the antidumping bill proposed in 1919. H.R. 10918, 66th Cong., 2d sess., 17 April 1920. *Congressional Record,* vol. 59.

_____. Statement and Exhibits Submitted by Senator Humphrey Concerning the Recent Dumping of Steel. 88th Cong., 1st sess., 27 May 1963. *Congressional Record,* vol. 109.

U.S. Department of the Treasury. "Antidumping Duties." In *International Economic Policy in an Interdependent World,* vol. 1, pp. 395–408. Compiled by U.S. Commission on International Trade and Investment Policy. Washington, D.C.: Government Printing Office, 1971.

# Index

127

## About the Author

**William A. Wares**  graduated Phi Beta Kappa from the University of Michigan in 1965. In 1976, he received the Ph.D. in international economics from the University of Michigan, where he is an assistant professor.